YOUNG VOICES

OF

LOUDOUN COUNTY

The Stories They Tell ...
The Lessons We Learn

Bobbi Carducci
Michael Carducci

Through faith
and imagination
a writer is born
Bobbi Carducci

Michael Carducci

Library of Congress Cataloging-in-Publication Data

Young Voices of Loudoun County: the stories they tell …the lessons we learn.

ISBN 0-9776613-0-X

1. Anthology 2. Regional 3. Young Adult I. Bobbi Carducci II. Michael Carducci

ISBN 0-9776613-0-X

Publisher: Community Voice Media, LLC
PO Box 564
Round Hill, VA 20142 -0564

Cover Design by Robert Howard Graphic Design

Community Voice Media, LLC
Round Hill, Virginia

www.communityvoicemedia.com

TABLE OF CONTENTS

ELEMENTARY SCHOOL

MIDDLE SCHOOL

MIDDLE SCHOOL (cont)

HIGH SCHOOL

Acknowledgments

This book has been in process far longer than most of the contributing authors have been alive. Like most things worth doing, it has taken years of preparation and a great deal of trial and error to bring it to life.

Along the way we had a tremendous amount of help and support from some very special people. The result is what you see here, a labor of love.

Our heartfelt gratitude to:

The wonderful young authors who took the bold first step on a journey of creative expression. Never give up!

Our families who are always there for us as we navigate life's uncharted waters:
Shirley who lives on in every exclamation point life has to offer;
Rodger who copes everyday with a world that refuses to make sense;
Elizabeth, my sunshine and number one fan during my brief singing career;
Harry who reappeared just in time for Christmas, proving miracles do happen;

Colleen and Darrell, Patrick and Becky, Michael and Heather, Kelly and Ray. Tyler, Jason, Rachael, Michelle, Vito and Andrew. Skip and Betty, Ed and Laura, Tom and Pam, Lisa and Tim, Dan and Shayna.

Our very special thanks to the judges: Tara Paterson, Dr. Twila Liggett, Jan Neuharth, Reese Haller and Thomas Haller, who shared their time and talent because they believe in our mission.

To Terry Henry, Deborah Henry, Kyria Henry and of course, Diana Keesee of Paws4People, who sponsored some talented young authors and taught us "that going to the dogs" is a wonderful life changing event.

For their generous support and encouragement:
Mary Covell and Linda Kelley - Delta Strategies;
Kim Weber and Ben Weber - Purcellville Gazette;
Judy Stearns - Purcellville Gazette;
Linda Singer - Final Draft Booksellers

Pennwriters, Inc and Round Hill Writers Group whose talented members inspire and mentor new writers everyday.

And to God, for all His blessings and guidance.

INTRODUCTION

Some people are born story tellers. They enter the world already attuned to the whispers and sighs of the wind. They stop to ponder the chatter of squirrels and the babble of infants. They not only hear voices in their head, they joyfully enter into silent conversation with them, eager to inhabit their world of possibility.

Others are nurtured into being by wise parents and excellent teachers. Introduced to books they become accustomed to the cadence of the written word, the magic of a story well told. Before long the brain begins to re-wire itself opening new pathways to expression. A writer is born.

****

We are proud to introduce the early works of some very talented writers. We are convinced many of them will go far. When they do, we will be the first to stand in line at a book signing and ask for an autograph. We will not hesitate to boast to our neighbors that we know them.

If you doubt my word or remain unconvinced of what we have discovered here, all you need to do is select a story and begin to read.

Be prepared to meet some strange creatures, Diar wolves live here and the eukaryotes are waging war. Just riding your bike down a neighborhood street can be a hair raising experience. There are lies and deceptions with which to contend and surprises in the garden to take you unaware. But please, don't stop there. There's more. In fact, don't stop at all until you've read each one and then of course the only thing to do is start over and wait for the next installment.

Some of the stories you will read are less than perfect in construction. The technique may need work or the ending may be a bit abrupt. We recognize these flaws and ask you to see beyond them and to applaud a burgeoning young talent. Just as we don't expect a young athlete to hit a home run each time, we can expect errors here too as new writers practice their craft.

Community Voice Media, LLC applauds all the young writers who participated in this book and we thank them for sharing their talent with us.

Elementary School

I learned that you should feel when writing, not like Lord Byron on a mountain top, but like a child stringing beads in kindergarten - happy, absorbed and quietly putting one bead on after another.
Brenda Ueland

The Life of a Crayon

What's in a name? That which we call a rose, by any other name would smell as sweet.

William Shakespeare

I would like to tell you about the life of a crayon. You may think it's easy, but it's not. I mean, think of all those little children who buy crayons, and don't have the words 'be gentle' in their vocabulary.

And I suppose you would like to know how I know these things.

Well first of all, my name is Turquoise Crayola. My best friend, Scarlet Crayola, (also my third cousin) encouraged me to tell the outside world about a crayon's life. And like I said before, it's not an easy job. Why just a few weeks ago…

"Come on, you can do it!"

"Help her up!"

"I'll get her wrapper."

Pink RoseArt lay helplessly on the floor, just where Cindy had left her, broken into two pieces.

"Here," Green Crayola said, "I'll get her top half. And you-" Green turned to look at me- "You and Y.G. get her bottom half."

Green is actually my mother, and is not only in charge of me in situations like this, but also the boss of our fellow crayons. Even though it's fine with the others, sort of a silent agreement, it embarrasses me sometimes. Right now was one of those times.

"Get moving Y.G.!" cried Blue RoseArt.

Y.G. looked up from making marks on the floor. "Huh?" she asked.

"Yellow-Green RoseArt, you are grounded for a week!" the very upset blue crayon exclaimed.

"Who do ya think you are? My mom?" the boyish yellow-green asked in a bored voice. "You're just my aunt."

While this whole dispute was going on, only the twins, Orchid and Lavender Crayola, realized that a human had entered the room.

At first there was silence; all crayons staring at the feet of the figure that had joined them. Slowly, our eyes worked their way up to the gigantic face. Then, as if in one body, all of us let out a sigh of relief. It was not three-year-old Cindy, as we all had feared, but her older sister, nine-year-old Julie.

Julie was a major part of every crayons life if they were in the Crust house. She was always picking us up if Cindy left us on the floor, talking to Cindy and giving the little girl 'lessons' on how to be nice to crayons.

As the eldest Crust child got closer to us, she noticed something was wrong.

"Oh no!" she cried when she saw what was wrong. Gently, Julie picked up the sobbing, broken crayon. Without another word, she took Pink RoseArt to her room.

Later that night, we held a meeting in Julie's room. The subject of the meeting was to decide what to do about our safety.

"We should run away!" suggested Gold RoseArt. "My relative Pink has been severely injured! Who will be next? Me?"

A few chuckles went through the crowd as Gold spoke his words. At the very back of the crowd sat Julie. She was holding Pink RoseArt in her hand. When the other crayons were done sharing their ideas (none of them as silly as Gold's), wise Black Crayola addressed the assembly.

"Long ago," he began, and everyone settled down. "Long ago, when Black RoseArt was still with us, he taught me everything he knew. All his wisdom was taught to me by parables he got from a very big book the Crusts kept on their highest shelf."

At this remark, he lifted his eyes from the crowd and looked at Julie. She smiled.

"Yes," he continued, "Julie would pull the book down from the shelf, and read it to him and me. Later, he would ask me about my opinion on the story we had read."

As the black crayon was about to say another wise word, rude Y.G. called out,

"So what? If ya got wisdom, tell us! Get on with it!"

Black looked at Y.G. for a moment then addressed the rest of us.

"The child is right." He said. "I suppose I shall confess. My wisdom is not enough to get us out of this situation."

After he spoke those words, I remember, remember quite vividly, that there was shocked silence.

Then Julie asked, "Why all the unhappiness? I can simply get my sister markers."

At that, there was another silence. But this silence was not shocked. It was a surprised silence. How could a girl of only nine have such a good idea, when their wise one was left saying he had no ideas? But that did not last long. Black smiled.

"Yes, yes." He said. "That would work!"

Everyone's excitement was growing. So Julie asked her mom to take her shopping, and when Julie came home, she was holding a box of markers.

She then went to her sister and said, "Here Cindy, if you give me your crayons, I'll give you these markers. Aren't they cool?" And those were the words that set us free. I remember the words and Julie's voice saying them.

Cindy took the markers and said, "The crayons are yours!"

So that's how it happened. Cindy now has her markers, and now we crayons are free of worry.

My name is Blue Marker Crayola. The life of a marker may seem easy, but think of all those kids who buy markers and don't put the tops back on...

Elizabeth Reid
5th Grade

The Wacky Jungle

I meant what I said. And I said what I meant. An elephant s faithful. One hundred per cent!

Dr Seuss

Last week me and my friends, Vasu, and Nick went to the Jungle. We went by plane. We saw lot of exotic plants. There we set up our tents. There was a thin stream of water running by. It had rainbow color water. But the water tasted the same like regular water

We went exploring the jungle. We saw a Cheetah talking to an elephant.

"I can run faster than any other animal but you just walk," said the cheetah.

Elephant said nothing and just kept munching the leaves. The Cheetah turned and walked away.

"Wow that sure was a strange talking Cheetah," said Nick.

"You can say that again", I said.

"That sure was a strange cheetah," said Nick again.

"Nick you don't have to say it again, I was just joking." We went on.

We saw a bear wearing a hula skirt and playing Guitar and dancing. When he was done we clapped. What a weird bear?

We went to the stream and we could not believe our eyes. A fish wearing a rainbow dress was singing and dancing. She swam to the other side singing in a low voice. It was amazing. It was getting late. We went to our tents and saw monkeys jumping around. We quickly chased them away. We had plums for dinner and then went to sleep.

Next day we woke up and ate mangoes, banana pancakes and grape juice for breakfast. Well we started walking and stopped by a strange tree. It was cooking spaghetti. Strange! We saw a tall rock with wild flowers on it. So we decided to jump down from it. There was a lion that ran away, he thought we were monsters. The sun was getting hot. So, we went back to our tents, and ate lunch.

It started to rain. We ate our lunch while waiting for the rain to stop. We got out, it was all slippery, and it had rained for two hours. It was late afternoon and we played catch the apple.

We went for a walk in the evening. We saw a gorilla hugging a cucumber.

Nick said, “What a weird gorilla.”

We started to walk back but we stopped at the spaghetti tree and ate some for dinner. We drank a cool glass of water from the stream and walked back to our tent. We said goodnight to each other and went to sleep.

It was Wednesday, when we woke up. We goofed around the tent and ate mango mush with mango juice. Birds chirped, the crickets sang. We walked in to the jungle and saw a bird with a fish head. Suddenly giant squirrels attacked us; we ran and ran until they stopped following us. We were out of breath. We went around the squirrels’ home so they would not attack us.

We had papaya and lemonade for lunch. After lunch we played hide and seek around tall trees. We went to Rainbow River and swam with the rainbow fish. But it started to rain soon. We rushed into our tents. By the time it stopped raining it was 6:00 PM. We just looked around the camp at the plants and ate leftover spaghetti. Then we looked at the stars. We all said goodnight to each other and went to sleep.

Next day when we woke up, it was very quiet. We had plums and water for breakfast and we started walking quietly towards the jungle, until we saw all the animals gathering up. They were talking about us. They started chasing us. We ran and when we saw a lake, we jumped in it. Suddenly beavers started attacking us. We all found sticks and swam to other side of the lake to our tents.

We dried ourselves. We had papaya and lemonade for lunch.

We saw elephants, monkeys and giraffes. But we had to be quiet. We played hide and seek, tag and catch the mango. Then we tried to identify the plants. We stayed near our tents. We ate dinner. Then we told ghost stories. Finally we put off the lantern. We said goodnight to each other and went to sleep.

When we woke up early with birds singing. It was our last day, so we packed and then went exploring for one last time. At last our plane came and we left for our homes. Captain said sorry he dropped us at the wacky jungle. We said that's okay we still had a lot of fun.

Deepa Issar
4th Grade

Tabbela, Cherry and Mr. Man

There are two means of refuge from the miseries of life: music and cats.

Albert Schweitzer

Once there was a pet shop at the corner of Cherry Tree Lane and I used to walk down there every day. Everyone who worked there knew me and I knew them, especially Kate, the lady at the front desk. She let me see the adoption list and walked me through the pet shop to see the animals. I really wanted to work there some day. One day, there were three new kittens on sale! From the moment I laid my eyes on them, I fell in love with them. The next day I found out the cats names were Tabbela, Cherry and Mr. Man! Here is what happened.

"Hey wake up!" Cherry, Tabbela and Mr. Man thought they were dreaming. "Wake up!" It was Tiger and Presious their neighbors at the store. "I want to take you to the Pee Wee Tree."

"What is that?" asked Mr. Man. "Is it here? In the building?"

"No, of course not! Would there be a tree in a building? Let me think...um...let's see here...NO!"

"Oh, I don't think we should go today, the rays of the sun will beat down on my puurrfectllly delicut furr."

"Oh come on Presious, is that all you ever think about?" asked Tiger.

"Of course not!" "Guys guys!" Tabbela said.

They snuck out of the pet shop and went in the woods.

"Are you sure it's safe out here?" Cherry asked.

"Oh, don't worry, there's trails" said Tiger. "We should be there soon anyway."

A half an hour later, they still weren't there yet.

"Are you sure you know were you're going?" asked Mr. Man.

"Course I do! We've been going there for years! Anyway, that's were Kate found us!"

That made the other three feel better. Another hour passed, and the trail ended.

"Face it were lost!" said Tabbela.

"That's right!" said Mr. Man. "There's the end of the trail."

They sat and thought for what seemed like two hours!

"It's surely midnight by now!" It was! "Hey it's a house! Let's go stay in it!" Tiger suggested.

"Look, we're sorry we never found the pee wee tree. It should have been right there! Really!" Presious said.

The house was comfortable and warm. The fire was going too! The cats fell asleep quick. The next morning, they found out who owned the house. <u>IT WAS KATE!</u>

"You're those sneaky rascals from the pet shop aren't you? Well I'll take you back," she said.

Later that afternoon, Mr. Man went out and to the door of Kate's office. She was having a meeting with other employees. Mr. Man was off to get a human snack. He heard them talking and thought it wouldn't hurt to be nosey. Those cats next to the Persian and Bengal, the Tabby, Mau and Maine Coon, their time is almost up.

"Two weeks! Oh no!" Mr. Man thought. "Tabbela, Cherry and I are those breeds! Presious and Tiger too! They must be talking about us." He ran to the cage to tell the horrible news.

"Guys! Guys!" he screamed. "If no one adopts us in two weeks, we're nothing but dead!"

"Aaaaahhhh!" Cherry squeeled. "We are going to be put to sleep?!" "This can't be happening!"

"Don't worry, we still have two weeks." Mr. Man said hopelessly.

"Hmm" said Tabbela. "I have an idea! First we'll start out small and make flyers and hang them up on the front door and who knows? When we're finished they could be spread around the whole town." So they got started.

"Good idea!" said Cherry. They had them all over the shop because if you look to your right, there'd be one. If you look to your left, there'd be one too! The next day, everyone looked at the signs in jealously.

"Oh what's the use?" said Cherry.

"Its' been one day!" Tabbela said. "Don't start worrying until about four days. Four days passed.

"WWHHAAA!" Only nine days left!" Mr. Man screamed.

"How exactly would they put us to sleep?" Cherry asked.

"Well, a shot."

"Everyone, I know the last adventure. It will be perfect! So we better enjoy our nine days while they last."

"Where will we go?" asked Tabbela.

"Out for a nice lunch" Mr. Man said.

"Hi! My name is Jerry and I will be your waiter" Jerry said sort of shouting.

Peaceful, romance music was playing. But then, right in the middle of the song, there was a weather report. Severe weather. The room was silent, but everyone was listening, including Tabbela, Cherry and Mr. Man.

"Later this afternoon, much of Arkansas will be in a severe thunderstorm watch. Possibly a few isolated tornadoes. That is all."

The music continued. Mr. Man looked out the window and laughed.

"Ha! Thunderstorms, tornadoes? That's just too funny! There's not a cloud in the sky!"

"Yeah! There couldn't be a more perfect day!" said Cherry.

"We'll just have to see" said Tabbela. "Changes in the weather happen fast."

"Oh sure, as if in a matter of five minutes we'll be looking at a pitch black funnel cloud" Cherry said.

"I didn't mean that fast!"

Early that evening, Cherry and Mr. Man got proved wrong. They were watching T.V. when all of a sudden there was a flash…boom…zzzt! The power was out.

"Couldn't be a more perfect day huh? Not a cloud in the sky huh?" Tabbela teased.

"It…you…well…ugh!" Cherry said stammering.

Around midnight, the cats were in for a heck of a ride. The winds were fierce and the cats suddenly found themselves out of the building.

"Mr. Man!" Tabbela screamed. The winds were over quick. Mr. Man and Tabbela were safe.

"Wait!" said Mr. Man. "Where's Cherry?"

They looked for a long time.

"What if she died?" Mr. Man said.

"Maybe she's still inside the building" Tabbela suggested.

They looked for a couple more minutes, and found an orange blob. It had whiskers, a tail and ears, it was in a tree.

"CHERRY!" Tabbela screamed.

"Aww, kitty stuck in a tree?" Mr. Man said as if he were two.

"Let's go back in, I'm cold."

The next morning, Kate pulled the three out of their cage.

"Time flys by, my good friends," Cherry said. "Yes, time flys. I'm afraid this is goodbye."

"Well here we are, the room of death" Tabbela said almost crying. Kate sat them down on the table and got out her sleeping tools.

"There goes our lives!" said Mr. Man.

"Ladies and gentlemen, enjoy your last few seconds of living" Kate said. The tip of the needle was touching Tabbela's back.

"Here it comes!" Tabbela said. One touch of the needle made her weak. Kate was just about to bing the needle in Tabbela's body, then...

"Kate!" one of employees called. "Computer message."

The cats' lives were saved! They were adopted! A week later they went to their new home. It was a big cabin with deer heads on the wall, deerskin for carpets and was loaded with fire places.

"I think I'm gonna like this place" Cherry said. They loved that place so much.

My favorite cats lived there with me for the rest of their happy lives.

Erin Taylor
3rd Grade

The Story of Buster and FuFu

Animals are such agreeable friends – they ask no questions, they pass no criticisms.

George Eliot

Once there was a dog named Buster. Buster was a shelter dog for most of his four years, which is about middle age for a dog. Sometimes the shelter would have big days where everyone was invited to come and adopt a dog. He would slowly watch people coming in and then coming out with a lucky dog. Well, at least he had his friend FuFu.

The dogs were always sad because every time they had an adoption day no one would bring either of them home. But that changed!!!

One day a woman came in and claimed she wanted a poodle for her son's birthday. The secretary pointed to FuFu, and before you know it FuFu was gone!!

Buster was so sad; he couldn't believe his best friend was gone. He would just lay there and look out of his cold cement home that became so lonely.

Meanwhile FuFu wasn't having a blast either. Mrs. Rhodes, FuFu's new mom was trying to teach her commands but she wouldn't listen. She just stared out the window hoping to see Buster. I'm sorry to say she didn't see him at all.

Mrs. Rhodes couldn't possibly give her son a dog that couldn't do tricks or even pay attention. So immediately she went to the shelter in search of a second dog. She looked at Buster who decided this was his chance. He sat. He rolled over.

Mrs. Rhodes smiled and said "this one will do fine" and she scooped him up and ran off quickly.

Buster was wondering if the end of this torture chamber called a car would lead to FuFu! As soon as he got out of the car, there she was...FuFu!!

And together they were a great present for the son. I mean how often do you get 2 dogs for Christmas; and they were well trained! FuFu was happy to learn some of Buster's tricks. Together they lived happily ever ...well you know the rest.

Caroline Abramson
4th Grade

Emily Ears, The Lazy Rabbit

Whatever you would have your children become, strive to exhibit in your own lives and conversation.

Lydia H. Sigourney

Once upon a time there was a little white rabbit named Emily Ears. She lived in the deep green forest with her family. She was one lazy rabbit!

One beautiful morning Emily's mother told her to help pick blueberries. She just sat under a huge brown oak tree and nibbled on a juicy orange carrot.

The next afternoon her mother said, "Emily, your room is a mess, so please clean it."

Emily did not know that her friend was coming for a sleepover, so she went to the storeroom and got out bright green lettuce leaves and delicious purple radishes. Later on, her friend came to Emily's house. Emily was surprised and happy, but then it struck her. Her room was a complete mess! She tried not to panic, but she might have to clean it in front of her friend! It turned out that she did not have to clean her room, but she had to push toys and dirty clothes into a pile so her friend could put down her sleeping bag. They quickly went to sleep.

The next morning, Emily's smart mother told Emily to help pick carrots. Emily just dozed off under a gigantic walnut tree. Soon the rest of the family had finished picking carrots, and it was dinnertime. Emily ate her main meal of berries and bits of lettuce, and asked what was for dessert.

Her mother answered, "The rest of the family will have carrots and warm milk for dessert, but you did not help pick, so you will not get dessert."

All of a sudden, Emily quickly hopped outside and returned with five juicy orange carrots. She gave each person in her family a carrot.

She declared, "I will not be lazy any more!" And true to her word, she was a very diligent rabbit after that!

Hannah Blasdell
4th Grade

Pirates on the Pacific

Where there is a sea there are pirates.

Greek Proverb

Chapter 1 - Set Sail

It was a dark and scary night at sea in the Pacific. The wind blew so hard that it had knocked a trunk overboard. Suddenly, I heard the tune of pirates whistling in the background, coming closer and closer until it felt like they were breathing heavily on my back. What will happen to the glue, suit, fruit, juice, and lunch? It was all so dull up to now.

Chapter 2 - The Truth

The truth, you cannot take the truth. Okay, you can. The truth is that the pirate's ship was going to bomb my ship!

"What? I thought that pirates didn't really exist" said a little girl.

"They don't," I said to her. "Where are your mom and dad?" I asked her.

"I don't know" she answered. "My name is Caitlin," she announced.

“Here, come with me. Oh no, there are sharks surrounding our ship, we have to call the rescue boat.”

Chapter 3 - The Storm

We are in the rescue boat, but storms are coming and we are almost out of gas.

“What is next?” asked Caitlin.

“I have no idea” I replied.

“We are sinking” shouted the captain. “Everyone, grab a life vest and help the kids. We must find a new rescue boat. Soon, it will be night and the pirates will be back.”

Chapter 4 – Alison Saves the Day

The pirates are back, but I have good news. We are on a ship that has sailed across the Pacific a million times. Her name is Alison. Alison is as beautiful as a flower, she is blue and white. She has a million rooms, some home-like and others as fancy as a castle. Caitlin and I have fancy rooms with two king sized beds each.

Chapter 5 - Oh No

As Caitlin and I cooked dinner, we heard a bang from the dining room. We went to see that the chandelier had fallen right on the table. We decided to have dinner on the deck. Luckily, on the way to the deck, I ran into the captain. I told him about the chandelier. He asked me for my room number, which I told him was number one.

Chapter 6 - Return of the Pirates

"Could all of these bad things be happening because of the pirates?" I wondered.

After dinner, everyone went to their rooms but me. I stayed above deck with the captain to look for pirates. I saw the pirate's ship; her name is 'Beauty'. There is a skull on its flag.

Chapter 7 - Caitlin is Missing

Caitlin is missing. I cannot find her anywhere. Where could she be? The whole crew is looking for her. I wonder if since I stayed above deck longer than she did, maybe she was wandering around on the third class floor. I will have to find her tomorrow because it is 9:05 p.m. I hope that the pirates did not get hold of Caitlin.

Chapter 8 - Bumps at Sea

Good news, I found Caitlin. She said that she was playing hide and seek with a girl named Kelly. It was her turn to hide, and Kelly never found her. The waves have been bumpy lately. The pirates turn out to be lost. In the Pacific Ocean, I wonder how they got here.

I thought about what Caitlin said a few days ago, "I thought that pirates didn't exist."

Chapter 9 - Back on Schedule

Alison is back on schedule we hope. It is night and the pirates have their cannons ready to fire. Wait a second; I thought how could the pirates be in sight almost every night, are they tracking us? We can finally see land.

Chapter 10 - Wrong Way

We do see land, but it is Japan instead of England. Caitlin is happy when she found out but is also sad because we have become such good friends. The next morning, Caitlin and I see her parent's ship in the distance.

"Goodbye Caitlin" I said to her on the dock.

She replied with the word "goodbye".

As for the pirates, I guess they are probably still lost.

Erin Bradley
4th Grade

Simon

Anybody who doesn't know what soap tastes like never washed a dog.

Franklin P. Jones

Last Mother's Day was one of those days that you never forget. It all started out with a phone call.

Dring, dring. My Dad answered the phone. While he talked, my younger sister and I played limbo with the telephone cord. When my dad finally hung up, he told us to put on our shoes and get into the car. When we were in the car, my dad told us that our mom had finally given in and gone to see what dogs they had at PETCO. He said that an organization called Second Chance Rescue brings some of their dogs and puppies to PETCO every other Sunday. My mom had gone to see if there were any dogs there that fit her requirements and had found one.

When we got there my mom and little brother were waiting for us. They showed us the puppy that they had found. His name was Simon and he was 6 months old. We walked him around and instantly fell in love with him. We all learned that Simon would have been put to sleep, because the shelter he had been in Tennessee was overcrowded. The Second Chance Rescue had picked him up and saved his life in doing so. We adopted Simon and found that he loved riding in cars. He took over one of the seats and enjoyed the view all the way home.

When we got to our house, we brought Simon into the backyard where we led him around for a little bit. Once we had decided that he would be OK, we let him off the leash to run around for a little bit. After a little while we brought Simon into the house. We gave him the toy that he had picked out himself at the store. Simon was lonely the first few nights, but once we started to let him play with all the other dogs in the neighborhood, he lost his loneliness. We had known that he was crate trained, but we also found that he was house trained as well. We took Simon through two sessions of training, where he learned basic commands. Simon is really fast and the only way we can ever catch him when he slips out of the house is when he stops to see another dog. Simon has also learned to jump the fence! Simon has a wrinkled face making him look very sweet when he wants to. He is a mutt, and the vets think he is probably part hound and part yellow lab, but the other part is a total mystery.

Seasons are changing and winter is approaching. Since Simon's hair is so short we have to buy him a coat. He loves to lie on his bed in front of our pellet stove. Since Simon loves to run, he makes my parents run with him almost every day. Simon also likes to chase after Frisbees and tennis balls, so we can tire him out that way too. Simon is really funny in many different ways. First of all he tries to imitate the sound of a fire truck with his howl. The sound usually is very realistic. Second of all he sits on the steps with us when we sit there to tie our shoes. It's too bad he doesn't have any shoes to put on. Another funny thing is he splits the night with more than one person. He will start in my sister's room and then around 1:00 AM, switch to my room or my brother's room. Once more thing is that he goes to the kindergarten bus stop with my mom and brother just to get a treat from the bus driver. This is the story of my puppy, Simon's, life so far.

Cara Broshkevitch
5th Grade

My Forgotten Toy

A man travels the world over in search of what he needs and returns home to find it.

George Moore

This is my story. I'm Teddy and I'm a stuffed bear. Listen up if you want to know how I got lost. I was about to move from Montana to New York, where we used to live before Montana. Maddie is my owner and best friend. Her parents hired the laziest movers ever because they couldn't afford good ones. When we were ready to leave for New York, Maddie didn't have enough space in her family's car for me. I was supposed to travel in the moving truck, but since they weren't the best movers, they forgot me on the front porch.

I tried to open the front door, but the house was locked and I had to find a place to stay until I could find my Maddie. I waited for the movers to return, but they didn't and it was very dark and getting cold.

I went into the woods behind the house to find shelter. I was so lonely, scared, and cold that I felt like dieing. I had never been left alone before and I never slept outside, except once in a tent. I was petrified. Maddie took me EVERYWHERE!! She was only 4 and was at the stage where she would have a fit if she couldn't have me with her. I knew she had to be so sad and maybe mad that I had to ride in the truck. When she finds out I'm missing, I hope she will go searching for me. I didn't know anyone who could help me so I decided to find a cozy and safe spot to spend the night.

I remembered the oak tree where Maddie and I used to play. It was big and had hiding places in the trunk and roots. I went inside one of the holes at the base of the tree. I didn't know what to do next. I thought and worried and worried and thought until I fell asleep.

Meanwhile, Maddie was screaming "I w-w-want my Teddy!!"

Her mother replied, "I know sweetie, I know you do, but you have Rufus too"

Maddie surprisingly remembered her puppy Rufus. He rose very quickly and started to bark in a playful way. They played together and that took Maddie's mind off me.

"That's the trick!!" Maddie's father said, in a low voice so she wouldn't hear.

The night went fast and the bright morning light woke me.

I sat up and said "Good morning Maddie". Startled she wasn't there, I yelled "Maddie, Maddie, where are you?"

I heard a hollow echo through out the hollow oak tree I had slept in. It was hard to imagine days where there's no M-m-Maddie here to play w-w-with and no one to hold me. I truly missed Maddie more than ever. I wiped my tears and scurried off to find something or someone.

After I dashed off into the forest deeper and I found a little pond, where I washed before continuing my journey. Later on, I ran into a huge grizzly bear that was sharpening his nails on a huge oak tree. The over sized grizzly was about the size of a bunk bed.

I scarcely said "H-h-hello..."

He turned around frightened and yelled "AAAAHHHH." He said "don't scare me like that."

Maybe he's never seen a bear like me before.

"I told you not to scare me!" he repeated,

"I'm so sorry! I didn't mean to!" I said.

He was a young grizzly; I was guessing about... maybe about 6 years old. I started whimpering, and I thought to myself, what should I say? He just stared and I could tell he was one of those young and wise guys that played pranks on others.

I got up my courage and said "I'm lost and I usually don't live in the forest."

He interrupted me, "No wonder you look like a groomed fur ball!"

I added, "Another thing you should know is that---"

Again he interrupted me and said "You have a zipper in your back!"

"That's what I was trying to tell you, but you keep interrupting me!" I told him that I was a stuffed animal teddy bear. There was a long silence.

I spoke up "We started out on the wrong paw."

"Okay, my name is... just call me Grizzly!" He explained that it was not his real name. When he was younger he growled at people who made him mad and everyone thought it was cute, so they named him "Grizzly." "Enough about me, how about you?" he asked.

"Well, my name is Teddy" I told him. I asked him if he had ever lost someone he loved and who had cared for him. I explained how my 4 year old owner moved away and how the movers left me on the porch.

His whole face changed after hearing my story. His eyes became big and sad and he was hugging himself.

He was saying to himself "Wormy, Wormy, oh Wormy, why did you become a Butterfly??

He explained he had become very good friends with a worm. They went everywhere together. Then everything changed when the worm changed into a butterfly. Grizzly explained he hasn't been the same since losing his friend.

The daylight turned into nighttime and he brought me to his cave and we slept really late.

And when I woke up he asked me "Do you want me to bring you back to New York?" He explained that he used to live there and needed to go back to visit.

In less than a split second I said "Yes!"

We were ready for our voyage and we were both exited. Grizzly said goodbye to his forest friends and told them he would return soon. Grizzly put me on his back and we began our walk to New York. As we were leaving Montana, I became very sleepy, but Grizzly wanted to continue on. When I awoke we were already in Michigan. He really knew some good short cuts. The lakes in Michigan were beautiful.

I was getting very hungry. Grizzly offered to kill an animal for dinner. I frowned, so instead we went from house to house, knocking over cans and picking out our dinner. Soon our bellies were full and I fell asleep again.

I woke up much later, and found a sign that said "Welcome to New York." Grizzly and I were so excited. Grizzly asked me to direct him to the new house. I thought they were moving back into our old house, so I gave him directions. About 25 minutes later, we arrived at the old house and they were there. The car was there, the moving truck, Maddie's parents, and Rufus, but I didn't see Maddie. I went up to the moving truck, and right in the front seat was Maddie! I ran up to her, but remembered I couldn't act alive near her. So I jumped on the seat and acted like I was there the whole time. She turned around, hugged me so tight, and ran inside to tell her parents. I looked back at Grizzly and winked!

Makenzie Conklin
4th Grade

Underground

Sometimes being a brother is even better than being a superhero.

Marc Brown

One day my brother, Jacob, and I were playing "dungeons and dragons" in the sewer near our home. (Dungeons and dragons is a game that uses lots of imagination). Players buy weapons, armor, and food then they go on quests to fight evil creatures.

You might think it's weird that two boys would be playing in a sewer but we do it all the time. We live in a small village and it's really easy to enter the sewer near the corner store. The entrance is a tunnel coming out of the ground; everyone does it because it's a very scary and fun place to play. We walked through the tunnel and suddenly slipped through the ground. We remember falling but must have been knocked-out because we awoke dizzy in a strange white room.

We were surrounded by creatures with large gray wings on their backs. They were helping other wounded creatures like themselves.

One of them walked up to us.

"I see you're awake. I was just wondering what brought you here and oh, by the way my name's Joe", he spoke in a gruff voice with an Irish accent.

"Well, uhh, uhh," I said with a groggy voice, "We don't really know. We just slid through the ground".

"Oh", he said, "I see. Well, come on lad, don't want to stay on ye cot all day do you?"

He opened the door and we followed him out. We saw many other similar creatures. Some were wearing vests marked 'POLICE'. Joe put on one of the vests. He looked really cool. He had long black dreadlocks, no shirt with his vest unzipped, loose jeans and no shoes. Joe led us to the door, reached into his vest pocket and drew out two guns and handed them to Jacob and I.

Then he said, "You'll need these. This is a pretty dangerous part of town. Well, now you're on your own boys." and he showed us the door.

We walked down a paved road for about half an hour.

Then we each felt a cool barrel on the back of our necks and a thin raspy voice said, "givvve usss alllllll yurrre money."

We completely froze and looked back. There were two creatures cloaked in black pointing rifles at us. Then we saw Joe and another policeman walking toward us. Joe and the other policeman each had a gun out and a weird blue tube.

When they got to us Joe turned to the creatures in black and said, "Hello my little snake friends."

Then each policeman raised their blue tubes and quickly brought them down on the "snakes" gun barrels. Then the creatures in black pulled the triggers on their guns. The barrels shook and then each of their guns shot an electric blast. Both policemen were hit in the waist and fell over.

One of the creatures in black said, "They forgot about the electric part."

Jacob and I shot the creatures in black each in the head. Luckily, Joe and his buddy came to.

Joe said, “Thanks guys,” and he introduced us to his friend, Alex. “We were coming here to give you theses jetpacks, because the only way for you guys to get out of here to your world is up”, Alex said as he handed us each a set of jetpacks.

We each said, “thank you and goodbye”.

As they walked away I wondered what these weird creatures in black are called, and what their faces look like. Then I reached down and lifted the hood.

I said, *“Jacob look!”*

Jacob turned around and gasped, then I looked back. There lying before us was a snakehead!

“Well now we know what Joe and Alex were talking about when they called them little snake friends”.

We stood up, and looked above us. There was a big hole in the ceiling with a sign that said, *This is floor 2 in the Gorgon village (beware no floor).*

“Maybe the creatures like Joe and Alex are called gorgons”, Jacob asked.

Then I said, “yeah, well time to go.”

We both turned on our jetpacks and took off. We were about to enter through the hole in the ceiling when one of the gorgons came up to us holding two silver guns with green bars on them and said, “you will be needing these sirs” and handed us the guns.

Jacob and I were looking at the guns. I shot mine at the hole above us and a large green laser came out of it and made it possible for us to go through the hole.

When we entered through the hole in the ceiling we gasped. There was no floor in front of us, and all around us where gorgons, almost all of them with a wing span of about 50 feet. Then we saw Joe, Alex, and 3 other gorgons fly through the hole. Jacob and I looked around in amazement. I kept thinking 'how did they make the room without a floor, and I really wish we didn't have to leave its so cool.'

Suddenly a huge ship flew by. The ship was a completely round, black ship with little green windows all over it. I caught a glimpse of what was inside the ship and what I saw I didn't like. Inside the ship I saw weird green snakes (just like the ones that almost killed Jacob, me, Joe, and Alex) and were torturing Gorgons!

"Hope you didn't see what was in that ship" said a voice from behind me. I quickly whipped around with my laser gun out and saw Joe and Alex.

"Those weird snakes are called Zorgons to let you know" said Alex.

As Joe and Alex flew away two weird purple creatures that looked like humans with wings built into them flew up to us. Jacob and I both got ready to fight them then. Then they drew scimitars.

Jacob and me shot at the purple creatures but they blocked the lasers with there swords. Then something very weird happened. Four lighting bolts fell from the sky one hit Jacob one hit me and the other two hit the two purple creatures. The two purple creatures blew up but Jacob and me were knocked out and awoke spiraling down a black endless crator without jetpacks. We both pulled out our laser guns and held down the trigger. A green ball started to grow on the tip of the small silver barrel. The light grew bright enough just in time too read a sign that said (in red), 'Beware Of Dragons.'

We fell trough the crater and landed on the back of a black European dragon!

"This is something I've wanted to do for years Jacob," I yelled.

Then I looked forward and saw a big pink swirling circle ahead of us and the dragon flew right into it. Jacob and I landed on the sewer floor. We looked around us and we were back in the sewer by our house. Then right in front of where I landed, an egg landed. The minute it fell, it hatched into a baby black European Dragon.

"Jacob look" I whispered.

Ethan Daffner
4th Grade

The Perfect Pizza

You cannot teach children to take care of themselves unless you let them try. They will make mistakes; and out of mistakes comes wisdom.

Henry Ward Beecher

Amanda Sarah stumbled in the front door. She had survived Monday, but it felt as if Friday would never come. Now she felt extremely lost. Her mother wasn't waiting for her like she usually did. Amanda sat stunned for a second, and then realized her mother was at work. Amanda spread out on the living room floor, switched on the TV, and started channel surfing.

Now she wished she could go back in time to remind herself to stay after school for CASA. But that wasn't going to happen. There was no such thing as a time machine that could take her back in time. Good thing mom (yawn) .....

"Hey AA!" someone whispered into Amanda's ear.

"Huh?" Amanda muttered, half asleep.

Amanda heard footsteps leave the room. She didn't care though. She would have been too tired to even notice if a bullet struck her head. Amanda heard the foot steps come back into the living room. She still didn't care.

Well, at least until that obnoxious person who woke her up in the first place took her Red Sox microphone and screamed, "Hey AA!"

That woke her up.

She sat straight up and screamed back, "Leave me alone, go away, can't you see I'm sleeping?" Amanda opened her eyes and looked up to find a staring Adam.

Adam was her older brother. He went to Bay Side High school as a senior. He has just gotten his drivers license, and a new navy blue convertible bug he bought with his money from working at Ruby Tuesdays.

Adam always called her AA because her name started with an A and ended with an A. Amanda called him bug boy because he had always loved bugs. Amanda thought that he had bought a bug because of his interesting them. But Adam said that he loved the type and their unique shape.

"What's the big idea?" Amanda asked, not as rude as before.

"I just wanted to tell you that mom won't be home as soon as she expected, and I'm not going to be here either. I've got another date with Ashley." Adam said.

"When will mom be home?" Amanda asked.

Adam glanced at this watch.

"In 4 hours, I picked you up some pizza. All you have to do is heat it up."

"Fine." Amanda huffed grumpily. She watched Adam walk out the door leaving Amanda home alone, which was a big mistake.

So I suppose you think everything went along as planned. Amanda heated her pizza, ate it, played a bit, mom came home from work feeling satisfied with her pay check, and everything was peachy perfect. But that's not at all how the story goes.

At 5:06 Amanda was feeling very hungry. She was also really cold. There wasn't anything a blanket could do though. It was the kind of chill you get when you feel like you are not important to anyone. That people had other things to care about other than you. That was exactly the kind of cold spell Amanda had. But, she was hungry, you have to eat something. So she sat on her little wooden stool and tried to figure out how to work the microwave. She decided to heat the pizza for 35 minutes. Then, she sat down to watch her favorite show, Sponge Bob and Sponge Girl.

Five minutes passed ... 10, 15, 20, 25, 30, 35 and finally the timer went crazy. Amanda opened the microwave and ... "AAAAAAHHHH!" The pizza had blown up!

Amanda had been so busy watching TV she hadn't been checking up on the pizza! The pizza was a mess. Cheese, sauce and pieces of the broken plate were scattered all around the place. The cheese and sauce were clinging to the walls of the microwave.

'What to do, what to do.' Amanda thought to herself nervously. She was afraid to clean it up because of the glass.

Light bulb!!

She would call her mother even if the punishments were harsh. She dialed her mother's cell phone number, only to get the voice message.

Now what to do?

Another light bulb sprung into her head.

She picked up the phone and called her brother's number. She explained the horrid situation she was in.

She heard Adam say, "I've got to go, my little sister needs me." Suddenly the cold spell was gone.

"Amanda what the heck are you trying to do? All I did was ask you to heat up your pizza and you blew it up. Were you really that mad at me for leaving you home alone?" Adam asked when he got to Amanda's so called crime scene.

"Adam, instead of yelling at me why don't you help me clean this up?" Amanda gritted.

"Listen, I stopped my date with Ashley to come here and help you and now you're telling me what to do? Oh joy! An 8 year old is giving me orders. Yes ma'am, on the double!" Adam teased sarcastically.

"I'm 9 you little Adam's apple!"

Amanda knew that was a sad comeback but she couldn't think of any other comebacks that would suit Adam. After all, it seemed to Amanda that Adam was perfect. He was nice, funny and really smart. Amanda could not bear the truth, no matter what Adam did, it always seemed perfect.

"All right, I guess we really should get working." Adam sounded peculiarly unhappy.

"Right..., Amanda said slowly. "Look Adam, I'm sorry I called you and Adam's apple."

"And I'm sorry I'm your brother." Adam replied with a silly grin on his face."

"Adam!"

"No really, I shouldn't have left you alone by yourself. It was my responsibility to take care of you and ..." Adam sighed and then smiled. "I guess I'm not as perfect as I seem."

"How did you?...How come?" Amanda gasped trying to figure out how her older brother had practically read her mind. Adam smiled again and laughed.

"When I was coming in the front door after your little pizza situation I heard you talking to yourself saying how jealous you were of me and how perfect I was." Amanda blushed.

Then the most amazing and weirdest thing happened.

Adam gave her a little hug and said, "If there is anyone to blame for this mess, it's me."

Amanda shared his smile then added, "Now we should get to work before Mom comes home and grounds us both."

"Roger," Adam said, giving a short salute in Amanda's honor. For the next two hours the two siblings worked peacefully.

Adam and Amanda were watching Disney channel when Mrs. Sarah arrived home.

"Hey mom! "What's up?" Adam asked. "Mom, if you don't mind us making something else to eat, well, the pizza wasn't exactly going to fill our stomachs." He added, gesturing to the empty pizza box.

"Sure," Mrs. Sarah said, getting out the meat loaf. "I was just going to do so for myself. Now, was everything fine here?"

"Yup, not a single pizza blown up, "Amanda grinned slyly.

"What on earth?" Mrs. Sarah asked puzzled by her daughter's unique answer, which was not quite as she expected.

Adam and Amanda laughed. Amanda knew she might not be as perfect as Adam. She knew she was still and would always be her brother's most prized possession of all. She never felt that cold spell for a long, long time.

Kelly Marie Davis
4th Grade

Rosie and the Enchanted Meadow

Tis distance lends enchantment to the view/And robes the mountain in its azure hue.

Thomas Campbell - Scottish poet

Once upon a time in a land faraway, there was a girl, who called herself Rosie. She lived in an enchanted meadow back in the 1900s.

The flowers were so lively they jumped and danced. The grass was emerald green and the air was crisp, cool, and clean. The animals were kind to Rosie. There were trees full of golden apples that were golden delicious. They framed themselves up against emerald green leaves.

She was an orphan. It was always bright, and sunny. Whenever the little girl longed for parents it would start storming. The flowers would wilt. The trees would keel over. The fruit would rot and the grass would turn brown. The wind would whip Rosie's black curls to what looked liked black wet sticks. The rain would pour down. Lightning would strike. Thunder would blare as Rosie would struggle to climb up on the hill. She would stand up and scream into the darkness.

"MOM! DAD! COME BACK! DON'T LEAVE ME HERE! I DON'T WANNA BE AN OPHAN NO MORE!"

The animals would flee. The storm would carry Rosie into the night. As if she was riding an invisible roller coaster. She would fly up and be swept down again. Finally she would settle down on the edge of the meadow on a high cliff. Below her was the city.

She would look out and stare at New York City below her. She saw smoke. She saw rich people and their little girls wearing fine dresses. They were decked out in lace and bows.

Although it was very cold down there it was quite nice in the meadow. She looked at New York City. Their polluted air. Absolutely no trees. The coldness and the chunks of snow that were on the ground. It would be a cold and dirty life for an orphan. She looked at the meadow and her little cottage. She loved her meadow and her little cottage. She was going to stay in that meadow. The horses came and carried to her cottage. The deer and rabbits followed her. Then butterflies would fly in between her. The birds followed her. It was like a parade.

Rosie picked some fruit and made fruits supreme then had some nice oranges for dessert. While she was cleaning she told the animals that they would need coconuts to make food tomorrow. The animals would have to carry her to the side of the meadow where the coconuts grew.

"Maybe we will get cocoa and make chocolate casserole for dessert."

The animals murmured in agreement. So the next day Rosie and the animals got just what they needed and had a perfect day in the meadow playing keep away. Rosie got in bed and the animals tucked her in. Her favorite bunny, Powder Puff climbed up on to the bed and snuggled in with her. Tomorrow Rosie would paint the city as a picture to hang in her cottage.

The next day Rosie went to the cliff and painted the city but when Rosie was done she realized the paints she had were too bright. She had crisp colors, not dull colors. She took a step and then Klutz, the clumsy horse, ran up behind her and let out a big NE-I-I-I-G-G-H-H that is how he says hello. Rosie was startled. She fell of the side of the cliff. Down, down, down she went. She saw the animals with shock on their faces.

She fell on her head and was knocked unconscious. Voices rose. People got help. Rosie was taken to the hospital. When she was recovering from her accident she noticed her colors were now quite dull and her face was quite pale. One of the doctors asked her who her parents were she said she was an orphan.

When she was out of the hospital she was hired as a maid for a wealthy couple and their daughter to pay for the doctor's bill. People were not that kind back then. Especially in a city like New York. The couple introduced themselves to Rosie.

"This is little Livonia. Livonia this is Carrel.

"Um. Excuse me my name is Rosie. R-o-s-."

"ENOUGH! I like Carrel and that shall be your name."

Livonia was quite conceited. She did not want Rosie to touch her very expensive things and she made that clear.

"Now I want you to clean the fireplace without touching anything, you will have to be much more careful when Christmas comes. I don't want you wrecking my old or new stuff. Now hurry up you reek like a wet dog. Ugh." Livonia held her nose.

Rosie took her ash tray and started to walk away. She stopped suddenly. She took the ash tray and dumped it on Livonia's floor letting it splatter on all of Livonia's stuff. She ran through the house and went to the attic and packed up. She had to leave NOW.

She climbed out the window and edged herself down. She was down by the time people started after her. She was on her way to the meadow. She saw the cliff. People were after her. The police. Livonia and her parents and the town's people. Rosie climbed up and stumbled when she saw the police starting up. When she got to the top she called out

"I AM NOT GOING TO JAIL AND THAT'S FINAL!"

The police came up but then Klutz came and knocked them off the edge. Rosie was home.

She lives on because in the Meadow no one ages. Whenever she is on the cliff and Klutz comes, the animals guard her all around.

Kathryn Ann Eaddy
5th Grade

Mandy Mouse Goes to the Zoo

Lions and tigers and bears, oh my!

From the Wizard of Oz -1939

Once upon a time there lived a little mouse named Mandy. And that Sunday Mandy and her mother were going to the zoo. Mandy couldn't wait. Katrina Kitten was coming too. And when they got there they saw giraffes and bears too!

Katrina Kitten saw a foresty path and a sign above it said 'Lions and Tigers'. Yes! Just what Katrina had been looking for. She skipped down the path while the others headed for the water show.

"Come on Katrina," called Mandy. "We're going to be late for the show!"

Katrina didn't answer.

"Mommy?" asked Mandy, "Where's Katrina?"

"Oh I'm sure she's right behind us," answered Mother Mouse.

"No," said Mandy shaking her head. "She's not."

"Well then we need to go look for her," said Mother Mouse sounding concerned.

Mother Cat heard them talking about Katrina getting lost and said, "Come on!" and she hurried back towards the aquarium.

"Maybe she went back to see the seahorses," said Mother Cat.

“Maybe,” said Mother Mouse sounding doubtful. But they followed Mother Cat just in case she was right.

She wasn’t and then they too saw the foresty path; the exact one Katrina had seen. But they didn’t know that. They also saw the sign that said ‘Lions and Tigers’ and they knew that’s what Katrina had wanted to see so they ran down the path and at last found Katrina! Katrina promised to never let her mother out of sight again. By the time they came out of the foresty path the sun was setting. It was time to go home.

All the way to the car and all the way home they talked about their exciting day at the zoo.

Megan Gingerich
2nd Grade

Lie

Truthfulness is the main element of character.

Brian Tracy

He needed to admit to himself and his mother: he cheated. His face began to blush like inside his cheeks there was a wildfire. His legs began to shake; he started moving his lip around.

His mother's head turned slightly and questioned "Come on tell me". His mom tried to use an easing voice.

"I got an A on my math test," he blurted out. There was a few minutes of silence.

"Wow you really improved…so let's see what was our bet?" she fingered through her purse. She took out twenty dollars and gave it to him. He looked at it then at his mother; she smiled. He forced out a fake grin, then she flung herself at him and hugged him tight

"Great job Nickolas" she whispered in his ear.

Usually any time for a 12 year old their parents are proud of them they are joyful, but right now the only better idea to make him feel better other than admit is to barf. She backed off still grinning.

"Ah your father would be proud" she said dreamily, her eyes drifting to the ceiling.

It pained him to remember his father, even in the position he is in right now. His face began to blush again like his heart erupted, spewing emotions all over his body. His mother turned and headed to the stairs.

"Mom?" he said emotionally.

"What honey?" his mother said looking over her shoulder still with the mile long grin.

"You should take this back" he said sighing.

"Why? You won our bet" she said looking at him strangely.

"Not exactly" he frowned.

She had turned around and came down the stairs slowly.

"I cheated" he said slowly and quietly, closing his eyes, tear drops starting to run down his cheek.

"You what, Nickolas?" she said softly.

"I cheated!" he sobbed. He dug his face in his hands. "I'm sorry God, but I cheated!" he whined.

She blinked at her son. Then she hugged him.

"You can't do everything right!" she said.

"Really?" he said sniffing.

"No of course not!" she stood there whispering into his ear for a few seconds, not letting go of him. "Not everything" she sighed looking at the ceiling.

Kai M. Hollenhorst
5th Grade

Howl – Howl – Een

The best hearts are ever the bravest.

Lawrence Sterne

On Halloween 2004, my friend Erin and I were trick or treating when we came to a hill.

Erin said, “Should we walk up it?”

“Sure,” I said.

So we walked up it and at the top we found a growling wolf

“Aww!” we said and ran down the hill. It was very steep.

The wolf howled and chased us into a haunted house. We stopped and the wolf stopped too, and showed us his teeth. They were yellow and his eyes were turning bright red. We were so scared that we walked backwards and bumped into a mummy cage. It opened as we turned around and it came out. I grab Erin’s hand and ran.

When we stopped running, we realized that we were in a graveyard. Erin spotted a black cat walking around the graves.

Then all of a sudden ghosts and zombies started to come out of the graves. We screamed and ran inside the house and ran into the mummy again. It grabbed us and put us in a hole. When it went away I found two shovels. I gave one to Erin and we started to dig on the sides of the hole. An hour later we got out! But we came out of the hole into the witch's room.

Then we spotted the witch. She had a green face, her lips were black, and her eyes were red!

Erin grabbed my hand and ran. The witch tried to grab me but she was too late. We ran back into the graveyard and a zombie got us and picked us up and threw us. There were two other zombies. One caught Erin and the other caught me.

There was a blanket in the middle of them. They put us on the blanket and tried to do popcorn with us. The last time it went up something happened. The zombies threw us up too high and we landed in a hole that one of the other zombies was buried in. Erin jumped out and then I jumped out.

We turned around and looked in the hole.

"I feel a chill going down my back," Erin said.

"Me too," I said.

Erin and I turned around and someone said, "Boo!"

Erin and I fell back in the hole.

"What was that?" I asked Erin.

"I don't know," Erin said. "I looked up and saw the ghost.

"Aww!"I screamed.

"What?" Erin asked.

"I saw a ghost up there. Look," I said.

Erin looked and saw the ghost.

"Aww!" Erin screamed. Five minutes later and the ghost was gone.

I climbed out and then helped Erin out. We turned around and saw the wolf. We ran and ran and ran until we found a gate. We helped each other over it. Then we ran to my house.

When we got home my Mom asked, "Where's your trick-or- treat bags?"

We remembered that we left them at the haunted house. Erin and I told her about our adventure at the haunted house and explained that we left our bags there.

Kathleen E. Huie
4th Grade

My Scary Bedtime Story

From ghoulies, and ghosties, and long legged beasties, and things that go bump in the night, Good Lord, deliver us.

Old Scottish Prayer

There was a time when I thought I was so scared to death that I would not survive. It was night time and my brother was already in bed.

My mom and I thought we heard thumping upstairs. My mom assumed it was nothing. Later I went to bed, but my brother woke up to get a drink of water. My mom helped him and put him back to bed. As I sat in bed I thought I saw the door to my bedroom move. It moved almost wide open! I thought for a moment that my dog who always sleeps in my room had opened it, but then the strangest thing happened. The door closed!

I thought longer about all the possibilities. Maybe my mom had closed it.

"Mom, don't close the door because Sam (the dog) can't get out" I said.

When my mom didn't respond, I felt shocked. I got out of bed and looked to see if the dog was there in his bed. When I found no dog, thoughts rushed through my head.

Intruder! Robber! Murderer!

I ran out of my room and cautiously looked for anyone lurking around. Thankfully nobody was there. I went downstairs and told my mom the story. Me and my mom put our thoughts together and realized that it was my brother. He was still awake when I went to bed so he probably did the thumping, and he probably was trying to tease me by opening and closing my door. I felt so relieved.

Ashley King
5th Grade

New York City

There is nothing like returning to a place that remains unchanged to find the ways in which you yourself have altered.

Nelson Mandela

This summer I went to New York City with my mom, my sister, my friend Zack, and his mom. When we got there we checked in to the Days Inn Hotel. After we checked into our room we unpacked everything. Then we went to bed. The next day I went to a restaurant called the Bagel Palace. The food was excellent. After we finished breakfast we went to catch the ferry to the Statue of Liberty.

First we had to wait in a huge line, and we had to even wait for three boats to fill up with people before we could go. Finally, I saw the Statue of Liberty. It is very famous. Then it was time to see Ellis Island. It was amazing to see real artifacts that doctors and nurses would have used! At the end of the day, the gang and I went to bed.

The next morning, we packed up and started going home. After three hours riding on the train we got in our car and drove home! I'd love to go back to New York City again someday, because there is so much to see.

Brian Knapp
2nd Grade

McGruff Camp

Life isn't a matter of milestones, but of moments.

Rose Kennedy

I went to McGruff Camp and I rode in a car. We brought our bikes to safety camp and we rode on an obstacle course. McGruff came to safety camp on his birthday. He got a bone from us.

Caitlin Knapp
1st Grade

Naughty Little Robin

A bird does not sing because it has an answer. It sings because it has a song.

Chinese Proverb

Robins call me naughty, but I'm not! I just get into trouble.

Hi, I'm Cameron (I'm a girl!). It was a really boring day. First of all, it was raining, which means we go to look for food. But I did not want to because it's raining and I'm not hungry. Wiggly, iggly, disgusting worms make my stomach sick.

There was nothing to do. I finally decided to take a tour around the neighborhood. I saw houses. Those are where people live, NOT robins. But I've never seen the inside of one! So I went and bonked my head against the door.

"Hello, is anyone home?" I called.

Lucky for me the door opened, just like that! I flew right in and pushed the door shut.

It looked like no one was home! Hooray! But then I had a terrible thought! What if there were eggs? Someone had to sit on them! Someone like me! I flew up these zigzag things called stairs. No sign of eggs. I flew down the stairs and came to a big room. Then, I saw something! It was a big white box with knobs. Could the eggs be in there? Carefully I opened the door. It was a place for storing food!

Just what I need! I closed that door and opened the other. The first thing I saw was ICE CREAM!!!!!!!! I took the top off and dug in! I was stuffed!

Then I saw them! No, not the ice creamy footprints all over the tabletop, silly!! The eggs! Oh goody! I sat on three. They were so cold! But I still sat on them. Suddenly, the eggs broke. But no chick came out. Instead, I was sitting on three raw eggs!!! I flew away real quick.

"Eeeeeeeeeeww!!!" I shrieked.

I flew upstairs into the bathroom. There was a tube on the floor. I got real curious. When I get curious, something bad always happens. I stepped on the tube. White paste squirted out. It went everywhere! It was like white fireworks sprouting up everywhere! Some left, right, sideways, too. When no more fireworks came up, I went into the master bedroom. I flew up on a thing attached to the ceiling with paddles sticking out of it and 2 strings sticking out the bottom.

"Cool", I said. I pulled the other one. The thing started spinning, fast!!!

"Not so cool!!!" I screamed.

Little bird droppings flew everywhere! Then I flew out the window, glass falling everywhere! I flew right back in though.

Then I heard something downstairs.

"Mom, who ate all the ice cream?"

I started scratching up these fluffy square things. I wondered what was inside them.

Then, a more high pitched voice said, "Mom's not home so you're supposed to take care of me."

I saw another girl with straight hair that reached her shoulders. She was wearing jeans and a white t-shirt that said, "I lost my homework, can I have yours?" She was holding a purple backpack.

"Rosie, did you eat any ice cream today?" the straight haired girl said.

"No, Louise," said Rosie. "We better clean this up before Mom gets home" Louise said.

"I think a bird got into our house." "Eeeeeeewwww!" Rosie said pointing to the raw eggs.

Louise sighed and cleaned them up, too. Suddenly, I flew into the kitchen.

"Bird, Louise, I see the bird!!!" Rosie screamed.

"Rosie get your butterfly net!" Louise shrieked.

Rosie waved her net in front of me. Louise grabbed it and furiously waved it wherever I went.

"Get her, get her, get her!" Rosie yelled.

She jumped up and down while clapping her hands. I flew into the net.

"Yes!" cried Louise.

"Hooray, hooray!" Rosie screamed.

I wasn't felling too good. In fact, I was feeling sick.

"Okay, let's let the naughty little robin go now," Louise said.

"No, don't," Rosie said.

"She made a big mess in the bathroom and Mom's room!" Louise said, "But we have to let it go so it won't make another mess,"

"Okay," said Rosie.

So they let me go. But before I went, I took a chocolate cookie.

"Good bye Naughty Little Robin," Rosie called.

At dinner that night I had an awesome cookie instead of worms. And sometimes I wander back into the house and ask Louise for the recipe of the chocolate cookie.

Hannah D. Lang
4th Grade

Surroundings From Somewhere Close By

Hold a true friend with both your hands.

Nigerian Proverb

I walked along the dusty dirt road that leads me to and from school every day. Today I was thinking about my family. To tell the truth, most of the time I am thinking about my family. My mother had been sick recently so I have had to do most of the work around the house. There was always my dad... but he didn't help out with anything. Whenever I tried to say hello or goodnight or even hug him, he would always stand there as stiff as a wall, not saying anything, absolutely no emotions. I have been trying and trying to get him to talk for as long as I can remember...but nothing ever works. Lately I had been having some trouble in school. My grades were still okay, but I was barely holding on. Today my best friend Malerie and I had a huge fight.

The oak wood door creaked as I slowly opened it and stepped inside. I spotted my younger sister Lark next to the stove, her hand clasped on the oven door handle. The smell of macaroni and cheese filled the air. Once again, Lark was cooking; she wanted to be chef when she grows up. Lark looked up from the rising heat noticing me. She stood silently twisting her index finger around a strand of her wavy brown hair.

"Okay, okay, I'll leave." I sighed.

Lark giggled and cupped a hand over her mouth. She was only nine, and she laughed at a lot of things I didn't think were funny. I left the room and found my dad sleeping on the couch in the living room. I could hear him snoring. I then went into my parents' room and noticed my mother lying on her bed reading a book.

"How was school today, sweetie?"

"Malerie got mad at me" I said, realizing how tired my mother's face looked.

"Why did she get mad at you?"

"No reason." And my mother didn't bother asking why again. She seemed like she had a lot on her mind.

"I'm there for you if you need to talk." "I'm okay, really," I lied.

I didn't want my mom to worry. She was going through a lot of stress, just like I was. I thought harder about what happened at school. The reason Malerie was mad at me was probably because I was busy and couldn't spend a lot of time with her. I was busy helping to take care of my mom and couldn't keep my mind on other important things like my friend. I brought my mother a glass of ice-cold water, hugged her and said goodnight. Lark served dinner, we both got ready for bed, and then I tucked her in.

Amazing, I thought! On my math paper from yesterday I saw a B+. I was so stressed the night before I didn't even study. I pay attention in class, but never expect to get anything higher then a C. I had to admit, I was quite proud of myself. After math class, I saw Malerie in the hallway. She ignored me completely.

I asked her "Why are you not friends with me anymore?"

"Obvious," Malerie said sighing. "You were not paying any attention to me!"

I decided not to argue. I was glad I finally knew the truth. I saw Malerie walking away towards some girls that were popular. I guess that's where she belongs now, and it was time for her to move on.

When I got home, my mom told me that her headaches were getting worse and worse. I asked her if she needed a doctor and she said she was fine and that she would get better. I said okay, knowing secretly that she was not feeling better, but was in more pain. My mother was strong and bold. She had always believed in me and now it was time for me to believe in her. Several days passed and my mother grew sicker and Malerie continued to ignore me.

My mom always said birthdays were important. Mine was tomorrow! When I was younger I had always wanted something particular. This year I wanted a miracle. That night I prayed that my mother would get well on tomorrow, my birthday.

The next morning, I stepped into my mother's room and felt her forehead. It was hot and sweaty, and my mother looked like she was in a daze. Don't worry, I thought to myself. She will get better. Suddenly, my mother looked like she was going to pass out. I reached over to her porcelain phone on the bedside and quickly dialed 911! I noticed my mom fall to the floor.

"Ahhhh!" I screamed. Then I began to cry. I heard a voice at the other end of the phone.

"Hello, my mother just collapsed on the floor, and I think she's really sick."

"Dad come here! You need to help!" I yelled.

He ran into the room and looked shocked.

"Don't worry." My father comforted me. I had never heard or seen him do anything like that before.

Just then a doctor turned to my dad and I and said "I'm sorry, there isn't anything more we can do for her."

When school was out, I adjusted my book bag and started on my way home. There was the same rusted brown gate with green vines twisted around it like always...though this time it was wide open. I had always wondered what was on the other side, and now I could see green grass untrimmed and stones randomly placed everywhere. Trees surrounded everything. When you first look at the forest, it looks so plain and boring, just because it is all the same thing. I know what it really is: a surrounding from somewhere close by...and I thought it was beautiful. Then I looked up, smiling at my father, and slipping my hand into his.

Isabel Motivans
5th Grade

Piggy and Her Friends

Love is all we have, the only way we can help each other.
Euripedes

This is a story about a pig who is trying to get some friends. She meets a bird, cow and elephant.

Piggy was working in her garden, because she didn't have any friends.

The next day Piggy saw an elephant, bird and a cow walking near Blue River rain forest. Piggy thought they could be her friends.

Piggy saw the cow first and said, "Hi."

The cow said hi back. Every day they used to play with each others things. Piggy had a friend! Piggy was happy.

The next day, Piggy and cow met a tiny little orange bird. The bird knew the elephant. Piggy was surprised to see a huge elephant!

Piggy wanted all the animals she met to be her friend. After a while all of the animals jumped in to the lake and had so much fun. Piggy did too!

"What a nice day!" Piggy said.

Gayatri Pai
2nd Grade

The Bermuda Triangle Adventure

Man's mind and spirit grow with the space in which they are allowed to operate.

Krafft A. Ehricke, rocket pioneer

One fine day, an aircraft carrier was sailing on the ocean. The aircraft carrier was U.S. Mega-Marine Carrier 71. It could hold 20 jets in one hangar, and it had six hangars on board. The best pilot was named Pilot Bradley Smith. When Bradley Smith was taking off, he noticed an ally carrier in the distance. He already knew it was there, but he had a mission to see what was on board, so the allies could help the mega-marine carrier with loading more fuel.

The other Marine carrier was called Mega-Marine Carrier 75, or MMC 75. Once MMC 75 got closer to MMC 71, people that were on MMC 75 were throwing refuelers over to MMC 71. As Bradley Smith soared towards MMC 75, he noticed some huge waves coming towards the two ships. There was also some fog right over the waves. Bradley Smith decided to land on MMC 75 and tell about the fog and the waves that were coming towards the two ships.

MMC 75 transported the message to MMC 71. Once MMC 71 and MMC 75 knew about the waves, they were hurrying to get MMC 71 refueled so they could get away from the fog and the waves. But they were too late! Now that the two carriers were covered in fog and big waves were crashing against them, Bradley Smith had no choice but to take off and use his radar to find another ship.

He was lucky because MMC 55 was nearby. He had to use his radar to find MMC 55, because by the time he reached MMC 55, it was already covered in fog! When he landed on MMC 55, he found that all of the men on board were lying down, looking harmless, though they did not seem to move, even if Bradley Smith tried to wake them up. He tried shaking them and pushing them into the control room, but everyone was too heavy.

Bradley Smith liked to be called just Bradley. Bradley knew how to control an aircraft carrier, so he had to use the radar on MMC 55 to find the U.S. Naval Yard Port Number 32. When he got the ship back to Port 32, he saw people on the beach and there seemed to be no sign of any fog to them. Before Bradley tried to go and rescue the other ships, he needed some help. But when Bradley left the fog, it seemed to him like it was only a big triangle out at sea. Bradley told his captain at the port all about how he rescued that ship and how it seemed to be a big triangle of fog out in the middle of the sea. The captain and most of the men that were at the port took all rescue ships and carriers to see what had happened.

When they got to MMC 71 and 75, they saw a huge, swirling vortex over all of the ships that were out at sea. Suddenly, every ship that was there was sucked into the vortex and into another dimension. They had found themselves on another planet and they saw in the distance an alien base. They knew it was an alien base because thousands of people had been sucked into a vortex before and had drawn pictures of the alien base before. But the pictures that the U.S. had seen did not tell what kind of base it was. So, the Marines and their ships found themselves floating in a huge lava ocean. There were burning hot balls of fire shooting from the lava. Bradley noticed a lava river coming from the ocean right to the alien base. The river could fit all of their rescue boats and their aircraft carriers, so they decided to come upstream with weapons loaded and see what the alien base was.

To their surprise, the aliens were there waiting to greet the carriers and the people on board the ships. To the people on board the ships, it felt like the aliens could see the future. The aliens were actually quite friendly! The soldiers decided to stay with the aliens because they seemed to be able to read minds. Of course, since they could read minds, they had a huge building that the aliens led the soldiers to. The aliens helped the soldiers to set up their beds. The aliens promised they would clean the ships and get them ready to attack the robots. Bradley asked what kind of robots they were. The aliens told them about a huge war that the aliens were in that had lasted over a million years. The aliens asked if the soldiers could help them with the war. That was why they were capturing aircraft carriers and ships from Earth. Bradley asked what planet this was called. The aliens said the planet was called Honrose.

The next day, they went to battle with the robots. The robots had already been all over the planet, but so had the aliens. The aliens were using ion tanks and X-Force satellite radio ships to battle and bomb the robots. The robots had super cannons and five red X bombers. The people on board the aircraft carriers and the rescue boats were armed with heavy-duty missiles, F-17 and F-16 jets, and one of each kind of tank in the world. In about six hours, the aliens had won, with the help of the U.S. Marines.

After the aliens and the Marines got back to base, the aliens showed the Marines how to get back to the vortex and get home. Once the U.S. Marines got back to Earth, they went to the President and told him all about the alien war and the vortex and all the things that they had seen on their trip to the alien world. The President put it on T.V., but did not believe the U.S. Marines. Not even the world believed them about their trip once they had heard about it on T.V.

The U.S. Marines told the President and the people who didn't believe them, "One day, you will go to the alien world and see what the aliens have."

Maxwell Pyle
2nd Grade

Beach Boy Ginger

Run, run as fast as you can. You can't catch me I'm the gingerbread man.

Classic children's story

Once upon a time there was an old widow that lived in a big beach house. She had one dog, one cat, but no children. One day, around Christmas time, she decided to make gingerbread men. She took out her recipe.

"Hmmmm, lets see. 2 cups of sugar, 3 teaspoons of milk, 150 milliliters of salt and shape it correctly." She put it in the oven and went to her room to rest.

Then, her cat smelled the gingerbread men getting cooked. She went in the kitchen and scratched on the oven door. The door flew open.

"Screeeeeeeech" went the door.

The widow and her dog ran downstairs and saw 4 gingerbread people running around. One in the corner had a beach hat, sunglasses and a swimsuit on. The dog got three and the cat got one. But who was left? BEACH BOY GINGER!

He ran out the door calling, "Ha, Ha timbers, I'm Beach Boy Ginger!"

The widow, the dog and the cat ran after him and yelled, "Get him!"

While they were running, the dog ran into the fisherman. He saw the Beach Boy Ginger and ran after him.

On the way he dropped his fishing pole in front of the farmer and he saw Beach Boy Ginger and started to run after him. Then, the farmer stepped on the milkman's foot. He saw Beach Boy Ginger and ran.

But, as always, he said, "Ha, Ha timbers, I'm Beach Boy Ginger!"

On the way, the milkman's milk jar fell off the cart! It startled the villagers. They saw Beach Boy Ginger and ran.

So Beach Boy Ginger yelled at the top of his lungs, "Ha, Ha timbers, I'm Beach Boy Ginger!!!"

Then, little Beach Boy Ginger realized the whole town was chasing him!

Then he caught a beautiful sight. A BEACH! He ran and hid under an umbrella.

"Yay!" he said. "Good news!" A pelican spotted him and Beach Boy Ginger hopped on its back and flew out of sight. Everyone ran to an airport and flew away. One person chose to jump out the widow and fly from a parachute.

When she was flying, she saw a brown cookie lying on a cloud. She jumped on and she fell through. Same with Beach Boy Ginger! They landed in a tree in a bird's nest. But then they saw the Momma bird with her babies. The widow jumped out of the tree and landed in a meadow of flowers.

Then she realized, "Hey! That gingerbread thing is mine!" She climbed up the tree and grabbed him from the bird. She ran down and said; "Now you are mine!"

She ran home and set him on the table, but did she eat him? No. She gave him a house to live in. But not just an ordinary house. A BEACH HOUSE!

They lived happily ever after.

Lara Reid
3rd Grade

The Little Hero

Heroes are created by popular demand, sometimes out of the scantiest materials.

Gerald W. Johnson

One day, on the island of Japan, there was a big tsunami. Every one was left homeless. On the other side lived a little raindrop named Little Scoochy Scooch. He was happy and wet, but he had one little problem.

Every time it rained, he went up in a cycle. He lived on a grass land on the coast of Japan. He though that if he blocked the evaporation, he wouldn't go up to the clouds!

And, Sunday night, it started to rain. He jumped out of his bed, took his quilt and put it over him.

He woke up Monday morning and found himself sleeping in the clouds.

"Oh, man," he said. Ring, ling, aliiiiiiiiiiing, went his alarm clock.

"Oh, no!" he cried. "I'm going to be late for school!"

So, he pushed open the cloud and ran to "rain school."

When he got there, his teacher, Mrs. McMuffin, said: "All right, class, take out your science books!"

Scoochy Scooch took out his science book and turned to the page.

But on the top it read: "Life Cycles. "

"Life Cycles?" he said to himself.

He learned all about them that they were good and gentle.

"Ohhh," said Scoochy.

And so he was never scared of a life cycle again. And, so in the future, he was called "The Life Cycle Hero."

Lara Reid
3rd Grade

The Surprise In The Garden

If nothing is going well, call your grandmother.

Italian proverb

One summer day there was a man. He had a son. One day the man went into his garden. The man went there every afternoon, but this time when the man went in his garden he saw a vampire. She had long black hair and long pointy fangs. She also had black clothes. She wanted to eat him.

She said, "I'll be your friend." But then the man ran away.

The vampire followed him! But, the man stabbed her with a sharp, piercing knife. She died. The family lived happily ever after.

Juliana Rivett
2nd Grade

Nine Years Later

Exploration is really the essence of the human spirit.

Frank Borman

It was a cold and windy day. It was also a sad one. Today was the day when Emma's father was leaving on a voyage with Marco Polo.

"Don't go," said Emma. "What about all those sea animals? You could get eaten alive!" Emma was ten years old, had brown wavy hair, green eyes, and freckles, yet beneath she had very, very pale skin.

"Emma," scolded her mother, "Keep a civil tongue in your mouth."

"Papa die?" said Lizzie, her little sister. Lizzie was two years old. She had blonde curly hair and blue eyes.

"David!" shouted a seaman. "Marco Polo's getting anxious. Come on!"

"Is Tom ready?" asked her father.

"He's already on the ship," the seaman answered.

Emma still didn't understand why her brother wanted to go so bad. Ever since he had turned twelve, he had done everything his father did. She missed the old Tom who would play with her. And now, her mother was trying to make her into a lady.

Her father put Lizzie down and walked on to the ship. Emma, her mother and little sister watched the ship until it disappeared. Then they walked home to their log cottage and started a fire. Emma picked up her book. Lizzie went to bed and her mother sat quietly by the fire.

Nine years later:

Emma was walking up to the harbor and noticed there were more people there than usual. Emma was now nineteen. Lizzie was now eleven. Emma reached her mother and sister right when a small ship arrived.

Emma saw her father! Right behind him she saw Tom! But why was Tom holding someone's baby?

"Father!" screamed Lizzie as she ran to him. Emma could not help but run, too. Emma looked at Tom. "You've been gone so long! Why are you holding a baby?"

Tom explained that he had been married for a year now and that the baby was his child, Jane.

There was a strange lady standing behind Tom. She walked up to Emma and said with an accent, "Hello you must be Tom's little sister Emma and you Lizzie."

Emma surveyed her up and down. She looked like an Indian because of her long black hair, dark skin, and brown eyes.

"Who are you?" Lizzie blurted out.

"Excuse me but where are you from?" Emma asked.

"I am from Barbados, and my name is Kit."

"Well, welcome to the family, Kit," her mother said, with a smile.

Things were buzzing in Emma's head like, 'Why had Tom gotten married and had a baby but not written a thing? Why did he get married on the journey? And why had he gotten married to some foreign lady?' Oh well she was nice, and maybe she would ask Tom all her questions tonight.

They all walked back to the cottage, happily grown into a big family.

Mairin Rivett
4th Grade

Dazzling Snowflake Falls

Challenge is a dragon with a gift in its mouth…Tame the dragon and the gift is yours.

Noela Evans

Once upon a time there was a beautiful dragon named Shimmering Snowflake. Shimmering Snowflake had an owner named Clara. Clara was a beautiful girl that loved horses and dragons. Since Clara couldn't get a horse or a pony, she could have a dragon. And this is the story of how she found the dragon, Shimmering Snowflake, when she was living at Dazzling Snowflake Falls…

Back in town, all the kids started teasing me. I got mad and told my parents I wanted to move. After two months, they finally said yes. That's when we moved to Dazzling Snowflake Falls, and that's where I first saw the dragon that I named Shimmering Snowflake. She had a beautiful white coat with gorgeous dazzling wings and scales.

When I first saw her, I was delighted! I begged my parents until they said I could keep her. Ever since then, we've been living there. We built our log cabin on the edge of the lake created by the waterfall. There were butterflies and pretty trees, and most of all, lots of glittery dragons.

Shimmering Snowflake and me looked around the pond and went fishing almost every day. Fish was my favorite food. My dragon's favorite food was salmon.

Since only I could see all the beautiful dragons and sights, I didn't have to worry about being bothered by the pesky kids in the village. To the people in the village, where the garden was, just looked like an old broken down barn. But, to me, it was a paradise.

Shimmering Snowflake and I loved to explore. There were apple trees where we could pick apples whenever we wanted. When it was time to go to bed, mostly I slept in the log cabin, but sometimes, I would sneak outside and sleep under the beautiful shimmering wings of my beloved Shimmering Snowflake.

Julia Simpson
Grade 2

Bastet's Journey

This world is not conclusion, a sequel stands beyond-Invisible, as music, but positive as sound.

Emily Dickinson

PROLOGUE

It all started one day when my friend, Epoligue Estajo brought in two statues of an Egyptian god and goddess. When the goddess came around to me I got out my journal and observed the statue quickly. I noticed some hieroglyphs on the side of the statue. I copied them in my book. When I got home I decoded them with my hieroglyphics book. I recited the hieroglyphics in English in front of my mirror. Suddenly, a cold wind swirled around me like a tornado. I tried to scream but no noise came out. Then, darkness.

1

"Class!" Bellowed Ms. Snakeroots, "Class! Please welcome Ms. Estajo!"

"Hello." Echoed the class.

"Hello to you, too." Ms. Estajo said cheerfully. "Now, as you know I am Epoligue's mother."

Epoligue Estajo was my best friend. The cool thing about her is that she's from Egypt. Her mother and her know a lot about their culture. So they stood up and told us all about Egypt. Then, they let us pass around two statues of an Egyptian god and goddess. The god was Re, the sun god and the goddess was Bastet.

When Bastet came around to me I quickly observed the statue. I noticed some hieroglyphs on the side of the statue I put them in my book.

2

When I got home, I decoded the hieroglyphs with my 'Egyptians Life' book. The hieroglyphs said BEWARE OF THE CURSE OF THE SOULEATER. I thought it was just one of those messages to try and scare tomb robbers. I recited the words in front of my mirror. Suddenly, a cold wind swirled around me like a tornado. It picked me up and twirled around and around. I tried to scream but no noise came out. Then, blackness.

I found myself sprawled out on a bed. I got up and looked around. I was in a house that looked exactly like the house of the Egyptian gods and goddesses. I walked out of the room. Outside I saw many Egyptian gods and goddesses walking around. I saw Re, Bes, Horus, Osiris, Isis and Anubis but I didn't see Bastet. I looked at myself and gasped. I was Bastet!

3

I walked around, very confused. So confused, in fact, I bumped into Isis.

"Oh! Sorry Isis!" I said.

I slapped my hand to my mouth. My voice wasn't mine! It was smooth and soft. It could sing a baby to sleep any day.

"Not Isis, child," croaked Isis. I spun around. Isis's voice sounded like Epilogue's grandmothers!

"I-I'm sorry. What did you say?" I asked.

"I'm not Isis." Said the old sounding figure. "Come here!" And she grabbed me vigorously by the arm. "I'm Epilogue's grandmother. You are Katie, Epilogue's friend, in Bastet's body. There is a curse you must break in order to return into your formal self."

"What is that curse?" I asked her.

"The Curse of The Souleater. It is an awful curse that will call the Souleater to devour the cursed soul. On Bastet's most treasured statue, there is a warning about the curse."

"And I read the message.... Wait! Where is Bastet's real body?"

Isis started to weep.

"What?" I asked.

"Souleaten. Her body has been Souleaten."

4

I ripped through the God's House, trying to find Bastet's room. When I finally found it, Bastet was there; just not looking alive. On 5th bed in her room, there was a limp, cold as clay body lying on the bed. I went to the mirror and looked at myself. Then, suddenly, a greenish blue light started to come of the mirror. Then, blackness.

I woke up to a blowing of someone's breath on my face. I opened my eyes. Right in front of me was a teenaged boy.

"Hello," he said, "I'm Tutankahmen. I was a very young Pharaoh. I died when I was only 18. I'm going on my journey through the Underworld. And you are?"

"Bastet," I said, "The Cat Goddess."

Suddenly, Tutankahmen (Tut) started bowing at me and kissing my feet.

"When I was alive, you always were my goddess. By the way, call me Tut." He said. I stared at him a real long time. Then I understood.

"So we have to travel through the Underworld together?"

"Yep." Said Tut, "All the way through. Through the bloody rivers, bloodthirsty monsters and, oh, the horrible, terrifying, horrific…" his mouth quivered, "Souleater."

5

So I began my journey with King Tut. First, we found the perfect cave to stay in. Tut said we should have a small cave so monsters couldn't get in. But I wanted a big cave so we could actually breathe. So, we got a standard sized cave. Our journey began the next day. I stuck close by Tut. He had the spells that kept away the monsters. The first monster we came across surprised us. We were walking across a bridge that looked like it was made out of thin thread and decaying wood. The bad news is we were walking across a river of bubbling blood. When we got to just about the end, a huge, slimy, purple monster that looked like it was made from slime, reared up.

"The Muk." Tut said.

"The what?!!!!" I practically screamed.

"The Muk," Tut said calmly.

Then, he muttered a few Egyptian words and the Muk turned into a kitten and flew into my arms. I dropped it and it jumped in the river of blood.

Next we came to a forest of pine trees. We walked in and the moment we set foot on trail through the forest all of the pine needles flew at us. Tut grabbed an emblem and threw it up in the air. The pine needles froze and dropped to the ground. We walked peacefully through the forest. We faced many other horrors, but then we made it to a sturdy bridge when we got near the end, Tut started to get drowsy. I saw why in a minute. Right ahead was the Souleater.

6

When I stepped on the last board of the bridge, Tut fainted. His feet dangled off the edge of the bridge. I looked off the bridge. Below us was a broken egg with two eyes sticking out. I tried to pull Tut's feet out but I couldn't.

"Take…Emblem" were his last words.

I grabbed a yellow emblem and held it high in the air. I could feel my face being sucked into the faceless hood of the Souleater. Neck, stomach, legs, feet were all being sucked in. Suddenly, I saw the Souleater crinkle up and turn into a pile of dust. Then darkness.

I woke up in my room. I looked at my clock, 8:23; The same time as I left. I began to feel sad and wonder how Tut was doing. Suddenly, in my mirror, I saw a picture of Tut.

"Thank youuuuuu." The picture said and silently drifted away.

Ashley Walther
4th Grade

The Eagle

Similarities create friendship's while differences hold them together.

Unknown

The eagle wanted a friend. He saw a lizard and he wanted it to be his friend.

"Friend"

They wanted another friend, so they looked. They went lower and lower as they flew together. Then, they found another friend. It was a mouse.

They got a pet Iguana.

They went to the beach, where they swam in the water, even the pet Iguana. It was warm and nice!

Jacob Zieman
Grade K

Middle School

Writing is the only thing that, when I do it, I don't feel I should be doing something else.
Gloria Steinem

The Sign

Even a single hair casts its shadow.

Publilius Syrus

Nothing exciting ever happened on our back road. The pace of our boring life on Languid Lane was completely predictable. The newspaper boy rode his bike from house to house at the same hour every morning. The mailman dropped a handful of junk mail in our mailbox precisely at 11:45 a.m. Mrs. Truenose, our elderly neighbor, walked her standard poodle, Precious, at exactly 2:30 p.m. and scooped exactly one poodle dropping from the grass between our house and the Smith's driveway. Even our school bus arrived on time. Life on our lane was a finely tuned and very predictable machine.

On occasion, the neighbors would display ugly porcelain lawn ornaments in the shapes of grimacing dwarfs and overly happy forest creatures in an attempt to bring some color to our drab existence, but it was a sad attempt. Everyone just lived silently on our street ... until the day our neighbors, the Stentons, decided to sell their house in the cul-de-sac at the end of our lane.

It was a crisp fall morning when that real estate sign was hammered into the ground. It featured a large picture of the selling agent — a woman with a plastic smile that stretched her face tight. Her eyebrows arched so high they nearly touched her hairline. But what made this woman so different was her hair. It was so unruly that tendrils of it billowed every which way. Her hair seemed to take up most of the picture itself. I glanced at this sign as I rode my bike down the road before school. The bright gold banner beneath the agent's face screamed, "Houses Sold by Buffy Serpentine!!!"

I already hated that sign, and I had only seen it once. I hoped that the house would soon sell and the sign would be taken away. But no one seemed to buy. The sign was still there — week after week after week.

Then one day I noticed something. Over the weeks that Buffy's sign had been in the Stenton's yard, the hair had somehow gotten bigger — like it was growing. It stretched outside the frame and brushed the air when the wind blew. This was most peculiar, but I thought I was imagining it so I kept on riding my bike.

Another week passed. The hair had grown out of the sign, and things began getting caught in it one by one. The first victim was the mailman. His truck's wheels got tangled in the long blonde tendrils. He stepped out and looked at what had happened. Confused, he untangled the mess and moved on. Next, a few stray dogs disappeared into the nest of hair. Then a few squirrels, but nothing anyone noticed. And the hair kept on growing, longer and longer, until it stretched across the cul-de-sac.

One day, Timothy, the eight-year-old from across the street, went bike riding by the sign. I watched him from the window, hoping the horrid sign wouldn't ensnare him. He had just passed the sign when the hair started to follow him, crawling under his bike wheels and twisting around his spokes. The bike stopped short. Timothy looked in distress as the hair started to pull him back toward the sign. I wanted Timothy to get off and run, but it was too late; the hair had already twisted around his leg. He let out a blood-curdling scream as the hair drew him into the whole of the frame. All I could see of Timothy now was his hand, stretching out for aid when no one was there. He slowly sunk into the bushy bulk of hair, and then there was silence.

Another week passed. More and more people were being devoured by the hair. But unlike the mailman, they didn't get out. Timothy's parents, who frantically searched for their son with flashlights the night of his disappearance, joined him in the evil mass of hair inside the sign.

Nobody believed what I said about Timothy and everyone else. They said they must have gone on a trip and would be coming home soon. I knew that I was the only one who could save all of them. But how could I risk becoming ensnared as well?

Thinking of a plan, I remembered the kudzu that choked the forests along the interstate near my grandparents' house in North Carolina. State workers had to spray heavy doses of pesticide to kill it. I wondered if maybe a heavy dose of hairspray and some sharp pruning sheers would be enough to defeat Buffy's dastardly dreads.

That night, I sharpened my father's pruning sheers, grabbed a can of extra firm hold hairspray from my mom's closet and got ready to fight back. The air was clammy as I crept down the street, clad in black, motor grease smeared across my face to help me blend into the darkness. I was almost there; it was just a few more feet. But what was this? The sign was quiet; it knew I was there. I stood stock-still; my heartbeat thumped heavily in my ears. Then I felt a tap on my shoulder. It was one single curl, tapping slowly in rhythm with my heartbeat. I knew that I must act now.

With the quick expertise of a hairdresser, I shot hairspray at my hairy foe and swung the sheers into action. Open shut, open shut, over and over. I kept at it, spraying and pruning, feeling the hair clutch at me, trying to pull me into the sign. But little by little, the hair began to freeze into place. I just kept on spraying and cutting, never stopping until the last curl was lopped from the frame. It wasn't a pretty haircut, but it did the trick.

When I was finished, a giant ball of hair lay in the middle of the street. It started to roll slowly down the road, with people jumping out as it gathered speed. First was Timothy, then his parents, followed by small forest creatures, stray dogs — anything that was trapped inside was now free. The hair rolled until it hit the storm drain over the creek, dropping inside and flowing away with the water current never to be seen again. I sighed. The hair was gone; everything was going to get back to normal.

The next week the house sold and the sign was taken away. In a strange way, I felt sorry for it; Buffy's head was practically bald — just pathetic chunks of blonde hair sticking out randomly amongst her unusually large and shiny scalp. Buffy was no longer smiling in the sign. She had this grimacing look, her lips tight and straight, and her eyebrows were so furrowed they almost met in the middle. But I was relieved the sign was gone.

I settled down with my book and finished the chapter I was on. As I reached for my can of soda, I felt a slight tickle on my shoulder. No, it was more of a tap. I looked down to see a single, blonde serpentine lock of hair, tapping in time to my heartbeat.

Kelsey Baker
8th Grade

The Girl in the Lace Dress

We are each of us angels with only one wing, and we can only fly by embracing one another.

Lucretius

Listen closely, for I have a tale to tell. It is of a girl. This girl was different though. The girl and I, we were close. Well, as close as she could get, though I still do not understand her and most of her ways. She was pale. Pale as the moon. She was graceful and silent. She was one with the shadows. The rain never touched her and the wind never beat her. Most would call her strange or supernatural. I called her my friend.

It was early in the morning when I first met her. She sat on the ground trying to gather scattered papers, though most kids kicked them out of her reach. Her long black hair poured over her face and her endless eyes held no tears or anger. They held nothing. Her pale, narrow face housed those eyes as well as thin eyebrows and thick lashes. I bent down to help her when she looked at me. Her eyes staring into mine, as if finding my soul, my heart. I gathered the last of her papers. Most were dirty and torn, but underneath this mess lay neat cursive handwriting. The letters formed words, which formed lines. A poem. I didn't read its entirety, because that would be rude without asking. Before she turned on her heel to walk silently the other way, I stopped her and asked her name.

She only replied with another stare. Then she whirled around and floated along the hall. It was then when I noticed her appearance. She wore ballet shoes and a lace dress. It was the kind of dress that you wear a corset under, and as she drifted away, no faces turned to meet her glance. I couldn't help it. Just watching her. It was like I knew her all along. She looked so familiar, though I've never seen her before. Like we've known each other forever.

The next day I saw her, she was walking with her hair falling over her eyes, though she tucked it behind her ear multiple times. I waved, trying to catch up to her, but she kept walking. I quickened my pace to catch up to her.

When I reached her, she flinched and pulled back. I calmed my expression and uttered an apology. She nodded slightly and looked back at the tiles. I sighed and thought as I walked with her. I didn't want her to be the way I am, but none the less, she is. Why does she show no pain? I used to not go to school because I stayed up the whole night crying, suffering. Why is she like this?

At noon I didn't see her head to the cafeteria. Instead I found her sitting outside in the overgrown courtyard. The courtyard was filled with seven or eight feet tall weeds, so the janitors never really bothered with it. If you brushed your way through, there was a boulder in the center. But no one cared to get caught in the thorns or wrestle with the tall tree-like weeds. No one, except the girl. But she was quick at it, and her lace dress never got caught. She didn't turn to look at me, but she knew I was there. I pulled myself up on the boulder with her. I soon found myself talking to her, about casual things, nothing important. She didn't flinch this time, but she shook her head and I stopped, laughing slightly. Her eyes glinted, but besides that, she held no expression.

I asked her why she never spoke of her name. She only held those eyes. Those awful empty eyes. Those eyes with no love or hate. Those eyes with no anger or happiness. Those eyes with no pain or hurt. Those eyes which were a dark night sky brushing the black deep sea on a silent night with a new moon. I couldn't stand it. I couldn't stand to see her so emotionless like this. My hand tightened to a hard fist and I wiped an unwarned tear from my eye.

She only paused long enough from writing to look at the tear resting on my finger and stare into my eyes like she always has.

"Don't be so mad at yourself. It's my fault I bear these eyes." Her voice was a soft whisper.

Like a mysterious wind across a field of long grass. She picked up her fountain pen and went back to writing in that flowing cursive font. Everything about her was so graceful. So beautiful. So silent. I didn't know why she was hated by so many. I didn't know why no one ever paused to say hello. Or no one held the door for her. It was so sad... So sad to see her like that. A ghost in her own time. Her whisper drifting through the halls. I didn't see her stop writing. I tried to smile, but no happiness came. I asked her what she was writing. She looked at her paper and then back at me.

"Do you know who I am?
Do you care?
I wouldn't think so.
Nobody ever does.

But if you are one of those few,
I praise you.
Because though you saw no reward,
You gave me your time.

Have you looked into my eyes?
I've looked into yours.
And I see pure waves of love,
Like a sea of silky gold.

You didn't have to share it with me,
But you chose to, out of your heart,
And there is a reward.
Let me share my gift with you.

Have you ever wanted someone to protect you?
To guide you?
To love you, no matter what?
Like, a guardian angel, right?

Your wish can come true.
Remember, you never were, and never will be,
Alone, unloved, or forgotten.
I am always watching you. Remember."

I stared back at her, letting her words pour into my soul, stream through my veins, rush into the tips of my fingers, and play in my mind. But before I could ask her more questions, she was smiling. Her eyes didn't stare. They shone. My hand reached for her, but something held me back. The wind played in her hair. In a flash of light, wings appeared on her back. Loose feathers shook from the wings, mingling with her hair. As I stared in disbelief, she brought her hand to my cheek. It was so warm. Her face drew near.

"Thank you." She smiled in a heavenly voice. The next moment she slowly disappeared.

As I stared at the spot which she left the world, I let a grin enter my face. My cheek was still warm and her presence was still in the air. I hopped down from the rock and made my way through the brush again.

Once I was in the school the bell rang and I stepped outside, not knowing where to go. I slipped my hands behind my head and smiled, letting the sun beat on my face. I knew she wasn't gone for good. She probably watched over me this very moment. The girl in the lace dress. My guardian angel.

Stephanie Fedor
8th Grade

Thanks to Tank

Thanksgiving, after all is a word of action.

W.J. Cameron

In this part of the woods there was a legendary animal on the loose. He was not extremely big nor was he quite small. He was not known for his claws, his teeth, or even his courage. No, Tank the turkey was known by all the animals for the size of his tongue. Why he could lick a kernel of corn off the ground from almost three feet away! But little did Tank and his amazing tongue know what was in store for them on this Thanksgiving Day.

Meanwhile, in quiet Peacetown, California, Charlie was bragging to his wife Loretta that this Thanksgiving he wasn't going to get their turkey from any grocery store. Nope, he was going to go hunting in the woods behind their house and catch the "perfect" turkey. He had to get a big one because Charlie and Loretta loved turkey: turkey meat, turkey sandwiches, turkey soup, turkey pie, just anything turkey.

So bright and early Thanksgiving morning Charlie and his faithful dog Goofball headed into the woods in search of their turkey.

Immediately Goofball took off along the path chasing an imaginary squirrel and proceeded to nearly knock himself out as he smashed into a huge redwood tree as he rounded a corner in the path. Charlie hurried to pick up the now cross-eyed Goofball and then carried him as he continued his turkey hunt.

Goofball's ears perked up as both he and Charlie heard a "gobble, gobble, gobble" up ahead. Goofball took off again at a frightening speed and disappeared over the hill. Charlie heard a "gobble," then a "splash" and finally a long bubbly "hoooowwll." Charlie didn't know what to think, but as he ran up and over the hill, he suddenly knew what had happened as he began sliding down the muddy bank into the steamy hot spring.

Apparently Goofball had lunged at a dodging Tank the Turkey, missed and plunged into the hot spring. Seconds later, Charlie slid headfirst into the spring only to see Tank the turkey staring at him eyeball to eyeball as he slid by.

"Help," cried Charlie.

"Hoowlp," bubbled Goofball.

Tank stood on the bank wondering why in the world the human and the crazy animal would be swimming in such a hot and dangerous place.

As crazy as Goofball was, he still had the sense to try to dogpaddle to the shore. After all he was a dog. He was almost there when Charlie reached out and grabbed him by the tail. Poor Charlie had never learned how to swim and was on the verge of sinking when Goofball's tail offered itself to him. Immediately Goofball was pulled back away from the shore and they both started to sink.

At this point Tank, who was known for his tongue, not his intelligence, began to realize that these two creatures would soon disappear under the water. He looked up toward the top of the hill and saw Charlie's gun. What should he do? Well, he decided to do the right thing.

He dug his claws into the mud and leaned out over the water as far as he could. Old Goofball's nose was about to go under the water when Tank reared back and made a huge "GOBBLE GOBBLE" noise. Then Tank shot his three foot tongue out of his mouth toward Goofball at what seemed like a speed of five thousand miles an hour! Goofball saw this huge pink slimy thing first shoot by his eyes and then wrap around his nose. Tank gave a huge grunt and then little by little started pulling his amazing tongue back into his mouth, at the same time slowly pulling Goofball who in turn pulled Charlie still hanging on to this tail to the shore.

Soon all three of them lay on the muddy bank, exhausted but safe. After a while they managed to sit up a little, Goofball on his paws, Charlie on his elbows and Tank on his wings. Charlie and Goofball rolled their eyes toward each other and began to smile.

Loretta heard the sound of feet on their front porch, and then saw Goofball, wet and muddy, stagger through the front door, tired but with what looked like a smile on his face. But with Goofball, you really couldn't tell. Next came Charlie, also wet and muddy, who quietly closed the door behind him. "Well, big hunter, where's this perfect turkey of yours?" Loretta said. Charlie and Goofball again smiled at each other. Charlie answered, "Loretta, honey, this year we've got the best turkey we've ever had. And HERE HE IS!"

Charlie opened the door and in strutted a thoroughly wet and muddy Tank the turkey. Charlie went to the head of the table and pulled out his special chair for Tank to take a seat at the table. Loretta could not believe her eyes. But before the meal was over she was hugging Tank every three or four minutes after she learned what a hero he had been to save Charlie and Goofball. Goofball was having a lot of fun himself throwing kernels of yellow corn high in the air and watching Tank's amazing lightning tongue zap them right out of the sky.

Yes, it was a great Thanksgiving and the first of many for Charlie, Loretta, Goofball and Tank who stuffed themselves with their new Thanksgiving favorite – hot dogs.

Maureen Howard
8th Grade

When the Eukaroytes Came to Town

Evolution is a tinkerer.

Francois Baker

Life for Billy Prokaryote was great, because it was so incredibly simple. He and his family, which included his parents and about 35 billion other relatives, lived on a soap scum ring on the side of the Smith's tub. The Prokaryotes were bacteria that had no nuclei, (their chromosomes insured this), so they were fairly stupid too. Their cell cycle consisted of mainly eating and sleeping. One day however, all would change; all would change the day the EUKARYOTES MOVED IN!

Billy woke up early one morning not knowing that life as he knew it would never be the same. He quietly snuck up the tub, so that he wouldn't disturb any of his 35 billion sleeping relatives. He was traveling to the top of the tub so he could think to himself. With that many relatives you didn't get much peace and quiet. When he got to the top he saw a disturbing sight. It was a colony of cells, but they were not fellow bacteria. These monsters were huge; they were 10 times larger than Billy himself! These things were slowly making their way towards the tub. So Billy screamed one of his favorite phrases –

"AHHHHHHHHHHHHHHHHHHHHHHHHHHHHHH HHHHHHHHHHHHHHHHHHHHHHHHHHHHHHHHHH!"

The huge racket awaked every one of the Prokaryotes, except for great-great-great-great-great-great grandma Prokaryote, who had gone through binary fission more times than anyone could remember, was always tired, exceedingly fat, and known for being a heavy sleeper. The other bacteria were very annoyed with young Billy.

"WHAT'S YOUR PROBLEM!"

"SHUT UP!!! CAN'T YOU SEE WERE TRYIN TO SLEEP HERE!!!!!"

"GEEZ BUDDY, IT'S LIKE 4 IN THA MORNIN!"

Millions of other Prokaryotes were yelling in despair because Billy had ruined their sleep.

"THERE ARE MONSTERS COMING TO EAT US!" Billy yelled.

This got everyone's attention, because the Prokaryotes thrived on simplicity, and the fact that something was trying to eat them was completely understandable.

"WHAT DO YOU MEAN SOMETHINGS TRYING TO EAT US???" echoed billions of voices at the same time.

The bacteria were beginning to scramble towards the edge of the tub to see the mysterious creatures that were trying to eat them. Billions of cells were now running around in chaos and screaming their heads off.

"WHADA WE GONNA DO!"

"WHADA WE GONNA DO!"

"WHADA WE GONNA DO!"

"WHADA WE GONNA DO!"

"WHADA WE GONNA DO!"

Billions of times this line rang out throughout the tub, causing it to tremble slightly, and making a small group, maybe 8-10 million of his relatives, fall off the tub. This loss went unnoticed for some time among the bacteria, because it took a while for them to process the information. The Eukaryotes notice this very quickly however, because of their exceedingly large brains.

The Eukaryotes, using endocytosis, consumed the millions of bacteria at a very fast rate. About ten minutes later, the Prokaryotes finally realized what was going on, but the Eukaryotes were beginning to scale up the tub. Quickly, the bacteria assembled, (or at least quickly for a Prokaryote).

"Uhhhhhhhhhhhhhhhhhhh, WAR!!!"

"Yea that sounds alright to me."

"Sure whatever."

"FIGHT, FIGHT, FIGHT, FIGHT, FIGHT!"

The Prokaryotes had hardly realized that now the Eukaryotes had arrived in their tub, and they were under attack by overwhelming forces. The Great Eukaryote Invasion #9,336 had begun. Soon, word of the battle spread by osmosis. Billions of lives were lost in this great battle in the Smith tub, although it would never be recounted in the history books.

"SSSSSSSSSSSSSSSSSSSSSSSSSSSSSSSSSS SSSSSSSSSSSSSSSSSSSSSSSSSS"

Mrs. Smith had unexpectedly snuck into the room and sprayed an enormous can of Lysol Basin Tub n' Tile Cleaner into the tub, and killed all the Prokaryotes and Eukaryotes in the tub, all except one.

Out of a small crevice, great-great-great-great-great-great grandma Prokaryote appeared fresh from slumber, to see an empty tub.

"O brother, not this again."

THE BEGINNING

Amy Armentrout
7th Grade

The Journeys and Adventures of Swift the Shark

Appreciation can make a day –even shape a life. Your willingness to put it into words is all that is necessary.

Margaret Cousins

Once upon a time, there was a happy young shark named Swift. He lived with his father, a Great White Shark, and his mother, a Mako Shark, near the ocean floor. Swift was a good little shark, but he had a problem. He didn't like to eat. It wasn't that he was not hungry, Swift just didn't like eating what he thought was poor quality fish. So, he decided to try to find somewhere where the fish were more tasty.

He asked his parents, "Can I go and try to find better fish?"

His parents, being sharks, said, "Of course!"

He packed an overnight bag and started for the more shallow waters of the open sea.

On the way there, he saw something in the water that made the water blurry, but he wasn't concerned, he was a shark! Once he got near it, there were fish there. He swam towards it at top speed, but ran into something. He wondered what it was, and before he knew it, he was all tangled up. He started biting it, but it wouldn't budge.

Suddenly, he remembered a friendly barracuda had told him that these things were called nets, and they would take you to the top of the ocean, never to be seen again! Just then the net jerked and started to take him to the top of the ocean. Swift panicked.

There was a big fish on the other side of the net who laughed and said, “Look at that shark—he’s caught in a net!”

Swift bit at the net harder than ever, and just as his fin reached the top of the ocean, he managed to bite a hole in it and swam away.

After resting in an underwater cave, he saw the fish that had laughed at him. He began swimming toward the fish, slowly and secretly at first, but getting faster and faster. When he was barely within lunging distance, the fish swam away. Swift swam after him. The fish obviously had some trick up his fin, because he chuckled as he swam. Swift swam faster, and the fish darted into a tiny hole in the side of a cave.

Tired, hungry and dejected, he started off towards a school of small fish. He zipped up and grabbed one in his mouth.

“Yiick!”

This must be the fish his father talked about that were disgusting. He called them sardines. Not interested in having more sardines, he began swimming slowly and stealthily towards a huge fish. He darted forward and took a bite. “Ugh!” This was the second worst fish he had ever tasted! He then realized the fish was dead.

“No wonder it didn’t taste good!” thought Swift.

After Swift rinsed out his mouth with salt water, he swam towards a coral reef. When he got near it, a big shark jumped out at him, and needless to say, he began to swim for his life. The big shark was gaining on him, so he began looking around for any possible way of escape. Just then he spotted a sunken boat with a small hole in it. He wasn’t sure if he would fit in it, but thought, “I have nothing to lose.”

He swam towards it at top speed, and barely squished through it before the big shark snapped his jaws right outside the hole. Eventually, the big shark left, and so did Swift.

By this time, Swift was very hungry. He looked around, saw a crab, snapped it up and ate it. It tasted very good, but the claws kept poking him in the mouth. There were more crabs around, but he decided he had enough crab to eat. He went over to a sunken boat and tried a nibble. No good. The only thing that happened was a mean old octopus came out and grabbed him. Swift bit the octopus, who yelled, "Oww!" and let go.

It was then that Swift decided to get out of that part of the sea and go home. He had a problem with that though. Which way was home? He asked for advice at the nearest seaweed store. There he found a kind old sea turtle who showed him which way to go. He started swimming home, but a squid started chasing him. Swift was near home, so he made a break for his reef. He got there just as the squid sprayed his black ink. He quickly swam inside and slammed the door.

That night at the dinner table, Swift thanked his mother for a delicious meal of tuna cakes and salmon soup. He now appreciated it much more, and was VERY content to have it every night!

Joshua Blasdell
6th Grade

How the Avocado Came to Be

Every legend, moreover, contains it's residuum of truth...
James Baldwin

One crisp fall day, Guacamole sat on the bank of the great river, skipping rocks, thinking about life, and watching the wind blow through the yellow and brown leaves. Suddenly, through the ripples he saw the people of the village eating a huge feast with wild boar and all imaginable varieties of vegetables. Then the image vanished; another appeared. The image was of the people of the village again, but this time they weren't at a feast, in fact they were eating very little food. Everyone looked thin and wiry; their cheekbones were very pronounced. Then the face of Nahuaque appeared and gave Guacamole such a look that Guacamole knew it was a warning.

Guacamole knew there had been a good harvest this year and a number of feasts thanking Nahuaque, the god of everything. He knew the feasts were great but it had never crossed his mind that they had been too great. Great enough to use up all of the food.

Shocked, Guacamole ran back to the village. As Guacamole entered the village, he found everyone talking about how good the feast had been last night.

Guacamole ran to his hut calling out, "Mama Rebushca, Mama Rebushca."

As Guacamole entered the hut, he saw his mother praying on an embroidered mat. She looked up as Guacamole entered.

"Yes?" she asked in a calming voice.

Guacamole explained all about the vision he had had. She didn't speak until Guacamole finished.

"Well, my son, we must do the only three things we can do; pray, make sure we have enough food, and go to the chiefs and tell them."

"That is all we are going to do?" Guacamole said in disbelief.

"Need we do more?" Mama Rebushca asked in the same calm voice.

"Fine, I shall go to the chiefs. But you know what they think of me."

Guacamole remembered that summer he had thought the world was ending and the gods were punishing them. He had felt the ground shaking when a tree fell down. Not knowing it was a tree; he totally lost his head and went screaming into the work site where they were cutting down trees. He was from then on the town fool.

Mama Rebushca smiled and said, "And I shall tell Queta. She is a good gossip. She should get the word around pretty fast."

So Guacamole set out for the temple to see the chiefs. As he approached the yellow stone temple he started wondering what the chiefs would say.

Chief Heciwa would probably sigh, rub his temples and say "What now Guacamole?"

As Guacamole approached the guards, he said, "I am here to see chief Heciwa."

The guard nodded and led him through a path lined with trees, up some steps, and to a door. The guard knocked three times. A minute later they heard footsteps and the door opened.

Chief Heciwa took one glance at Guacamole, sighed, rubbed his temples and said, “What now Guacamole?”

Guacamole for the second time that day told his story. When he finished, the chief started to laugh.

“Do you really expect me to believe that? The earth coming to an end, shortage of food, really!”

Guacamole sighed and tried once more.

“Please, you have to believe me.”

“I am sorry, but I have to go get ready for the feast now. Don’t bother me anymore.” And with that, Chief Heciwa shut the door.

Guacamole walked away gloomily. When he stopped in front of his hut he decided that the only way to keep the village from starving was to find the god’s dwelling place.

“Mama Rebushca,” Guacamole said as he entered the hut, “The chief would not listen to me. So I have decided to leave tomorrow to find Nahuaque’s dwelling place.”

Mama Rebushca looked up at Guacamole with her peaceful eyes and said, “If that is what you must do my son, then you must go.”

Guacamole knew that his journey would be long. So that night he packed lightweight food that would not spoil quickly, and a thin warm blanket.

The next day Mama Rebushca and Guacamole got up before the sun. They said their prayers and ate some breakfast. Then Guacamole strapped the food and blanket to his back and set off to find Nahuaque’s dwelling place.

The going was easy at first; he just followed the path from the city. But the further he got from the city the harder the going got. Many moons later, Guacamole sat by a river praying to the gods to help him to find some food, since he had run out. As soon as Guacamole was finished he continued on. He walked for about an hour when he started to notice that the air was getting misty. Then suddenly, as if by magic, a tree appeared with dark green fruit hanging from it.

As Guacamole approached the tree he noticed two things. First, the tree was ten times the size it had seemed to be through the mist. And second, there were millions of dark green fruit. Guacamole picked a fruit and found that it's skin was leathery, but when peeled it with his stone knife; there was a soft, light green filling. It tasted like a creamy bit of mild lettuce.

Guacamole fell to his knees and thanked Nahuaque. Guacamole gathered some seeds and many fruits and started back to the city. By the time Guacamole started recognizing the landmarks, four moons had passed and he knew the people of the city would be out of food. Guacamole quickened his step, seeing the city materialize as he got closer.

Soon Guacamole was running. He could just see his hut: 30 feet, 20 feet, 10 feet, right in front of him.

"Mama Rebushca!" Guacamole yelled as he entered the hut.

Mamma Rebushca gave her son a huge hug and said, "Thank the gods you're back! Did you find the dwelling place?"

"No, I don't think any mortal can enter the dwelling place of a god. But I found a magical tree that has a fruit I have never tasted. I brought back some seeds and fruit from this tree, I believe that it was sent by the gods."

Guacamole showed the fruit to his mother.

Mama Rebushca told Guacamole about how the people had run out of food.

"Even Chief Heciwa came to see you a moon after you left, to say that he was sorry," she said.

For a minute Guacamole just stood there. Then, as if someone had given him a command, Guacamole went outside and planted the seeds from the tree. He went back in to the hut and told Mama Rebushca all about his trip as they shared some slices of the fruit. A couple minutes later, Guacamole heard many people cheering. Wondering what was going on, Guacamole ran out of the hut. What he saw he couldn't believe.

A few minutes ago there was a mound of dirt where Guacamole had planted the seeds. Now there was a towering tree filled with green fruits. Guacamole ran to gather fruits to bring to Mama Rebushca.

Together, Guacamole and Mama Rebushca made a paste with peppers and spices, to share with everyone. They decided to call the paste guacamole.

And that is how the avocado and guacamole came to be.

Emily Calley
8th Grade

Shrimp and the Hurricane

It is one thing to show a man he is in error, and another to put him in possession of the truth.

John Locke

The story that I am about to tell you takes place in an ant kingdom in the land of Malimbar. This kingdom is located on a beautiful hillside covered in daisies. It is called Albyatos after the first ant king. The entrance is a secret known only to the ants and myself but I will tell you because I trust you completely. First, you must find a special daisy with six petals instead of five, and then you must eat a palpyar leaf (these can be bought from Madam Zelinska in the city of Krutos). This leaf will shrink you to the size of an ant. All you have to do then is climb inside the daisy with six petals (it has been hollowed out for use as an entrance) and keep going until you reach Albyatos. You must follow my directions exactly or you will never reach this amazing place.

Normally Albyatos is a busy place with ants running around everywhere doing business and visiting with friends. However, a respectable ant by the name of Maybar had just returned from his outside holiday. Maybar, on his return, went immediately to the king bearing bad news.

"Your Highness, I am afraid we have a problem," said Maybar gravely. "A hurricane is heading this way fast."

In Malimbar, hurricanes are very penetrating and if one hit Albyatos, it would flood the kingdom and everyone would drown.

"This is not good, not good at all!" said the king. "Hurry, we must gather the Great Council to tell them the news and come up with a plan of action."

The council, once gathered, was told the news. Immediately they all started talking at the same time.

It became so confusing that the king yelled, "QUIET!!" Everyone immediately shut up.

"Okay, we need to come up with a plan," said the king.

The councilmen went into a huddle and started whispering to each other in quiet, hurried voices. Finally, when they quit talking, the senior councilman stepped forward.

"We have decided that we should ask for a brave volunteer to go and talk to the hurricane and persuade it to stay away from here," said the councilman.

"That sounds like a good plan to me," said the king. They signaled the horn bearer to call a meeting for all of the ants in the kingdom.

When all of the ants had gathered in front of the king's castle he spoke, "We have called you here today for a very grave reason indeed. There is a hurricane approaching and we need a volunteer to go out and talk to the hurricane to persuade it to stay away from here."

Only one ant volunteered. His name was Shrimp. Well, actually his name was Harold but everyone called him Shrimp because he was very tiny. Everyone just laughed at him because they didn't believe that he could do anything, let alone stop a hurricane. The king, who believed that all hope was lost, told the ants to prepare for a hurricane.

Alone and embarrassed, Shrimp set out on a journey to stop the hurricane by himself.

"I'll show them," he said. "I'll stop this hurricane and then they will all look up to me as a hero instead of just as a shrimp."

The only things that he brought with him were provisions for his journey, an umbrella and a magical piece of Swiss cheese. He didn't know if these would come in handy but he brought them anyway. He set out in the direction of the hurricane.

After walking for a few days, Shrimp finally found the hurricane. It was moving along at fifty miles an hour and it was all Shrimp could do to stay on the ground. When he got up close, he realized that this hurricane was a baby. It was very odd to him because baby hurricanes usually stay in the Crayman Ocean. He got her to stay still and calm down a little bit (all hurricanes are girls until they reach a certain age). Once he had done this he started talking to the hurricane and found out that her name was Mila. Mila was very sad because she had gotten lost and couldn't find her way home. Shrimp knew her home had to be the Crayman Ocean because he had read about hurricanes before he left the kingdom.

"I will tell you where to go if you take this umbrella to stop your rain from falling on the different kingdoms in the area," said Shrimp as he handed the umbrella to Mila.

"Here, take this too, and put all of your wind into the holes. It is a magical piece of Swiss cheese."

"Okay," said Mila. "Thank you very much."

"First, you must go due west to the great big hill and look around. Next, you need to look for a great big stretch of blue water. Finally, you have to head for the water and when you get there you will be home," said Shrimp. "Oh, and you can come and visit me whenever you want just as long as you remember to bring the umbrella and the cheese," he added.

"I will. Good-Bye!" said Mila, happy to be going home. With that, they both headed off home in extremely good moods.

When Shrimp got back to Albyatos, he told everyone what he had done. No one believed him and they all went about preparing for the hurricane to come. Shrimp went back to moping around and being ridiculed for his size.

Mila's parents were overjoyed to see her and allowed her to go and visit Shrimp in Albyatos. When Mila got there she rang the little door bell that Shrimp had told her about.

Her arrival made everyone realize that Shrimp had told them the truth. They all considered him a hero and he was made a councilmember. This made him very happy. Mila went back to visit with Shrimp many times and she always remembered to use the umbrella to protect Shrimp and the other ants.

From then on the hurricanes and the ants were the best of friends and Shrimp was never laughed at again.

Kaitlyn Fillmore
8th Grade

Popularity Bites

True happiness consists not in the multitude of friends, but in their worth and choice.

Samuel Johnston

"Mom!" I screamed. "Is the popcorn ready yet? The girls will be here any minute and don't forget the extra butter!" I added.

"Kali calm down it's only 6:45 and I'm adding the extra butter right now!" She answered.

"Well hurry up! This has to be the slumber party of the century! If anything goes wrong I won't be able to show my face at school! The popular girls are coming over!" I blurted back as I rushed from room to room trying to make my dull old house look as cool as possible.

The pictures were lopsided the pillows were on the floor things needed to be dusted there was so much to do and so little time. I was still trying to get over the fact that I Kali Commins was going to have the In Crowd sleep over!

As I set up the basement for the awesome party I was about to have, I smelled the most disgusting, dreadful stench that I had ever smelled! It smelled of rotten eggs and moldy meat. This was a familiar smell I had smelled this stench before. I whirled around to find my brother in the basement doorway.

"You!" I yelled. "Did you have a burrito for dinner again? And what are you doing here any way? I thought you were sleeping over at Brains house tonight."

"He got strep throat." He replied as a smirk came across his face.

"Well do something you're not staying here while my friends are here!" I screamed back at him as I rushed over to open the basement door to get some fresh air.

Just then the faint sound of the door bell came up stairs. "They're here early!" I said to myself then I turned to my brother and paused for a second, waiting for him to go to his room and make himself invisible. When he didn't turn to leave I told him "get lost pest, my friends are here!"

Quickly I pushed him aside and ran up the stairs to answer the door. When I reached the door I opened it to find that all the girls had arrived at once already dressed n their fluorescent velvet pajamas.

"Hey come on in!" I said.

"Oh what took you so long? I'm freezing!" the tallest one Taffy replied as she pushed past me and threw her sleeping bag on the couch. The rest of the girls followed behind her and plopped all their bags over the living room floor and sofa.

"So ... what do you want to do?" I asked. "I got a few new CDs want to go listen to them in my room." I said trying to stall them as the basement aired out.

"Na, I heard your basement has a plasma screen TV." Nicole said.

"And Betsy said you have some cool nail polish." Katy chimed in.

"Well OK sure let's go the basement is this way." I told them as I pointed to the big yellow door at the end of the hallway. "So much for letting the basement air out." I muttered to myself as we walked down the narrow stairway.

When it came time to layout our sleeping bags, I saw that all the girl's bags had faces of celebrities on them or pictures of make-up while mine had Hello Kitty all over it.

As I turned to go get a different sleeping bag Taffy asked, “Where are you going?”

“Oh well …?” I sputtered out.

She cut me off in a inquiring laughing manner, “Is that Hello Kitty on your sleeping bag?” That got the whole group laughing and I didn’t get a chance to say anything.

After the girls recovered from their giggle tantrum, we climbed into our sleeping bags and started to tell scary ghost stories. I told of a long green monster with sharp teeth that slide through dark places that killed everyone in site. All of us freaked out and decided to go to sleep but when Taffy got into her bag she thought she saw something slither in front of her. We all decided to curl up in our sleeping bag next to each other for security. I was so excited that the slumber party was going well … well enough.

I fell into a peaceful dreamy sleep. But soon I woke to a high pitched scream bursting out next to my ear. I was still half asleep, so for a minute I just stared at Taffy before really realizing what was happening. Nicole and Jessica were both awake and soon they all were screaming and fussing with their sleeping bags, Nicole was even jumping up and down.

“What’s wrong?” I asked sleepily.

“There … there there’s a monster! The one you told us about!” Jessica stammered. “And it was in my sleeping bag!” yelled Taffy.

“Well clam down.” I tried to coax them. “Where did it go?” I added.

“We don’t know!” they all screamed in unison.

“Well first of all” I said “the monster I told you about doesn’t exist and second of all it could be a snake so don’t step on it.”

“Quick turn on the lights” somebody ordered. I ran over and flipped the light switch and suddenly the room filled with color and light. I searched franticly for anything that looked like a snake. The girls panicked, their faces were bright red and you could see the fear in their eyes. The fearless, rude, cool girls I knew had suddenly transformed into scared small little girls I had never met.

I knew my sleep over was ruined unless I did something drastic. Suddenly I caught sight of the little green snake that had ruined my party. All of a sudden I knew what I had to do. I gulped and tried to swallow the sobs and tears that were about to come. Quickly I grabbed the snake, my friends screaming in horror. I felt a sharp pain in my hand but ignored it. I rushed to the door; I knew I had to save the day in order to ever be able to show my face again. I felt like Super Woman, I opened the door and with one small toss the snake went flying and the room was silent for a minute.

I looked at my hand and saw bite marks. All of a sudden the girls ran over to me cheering and yelling with amazement.

"Oh my gosh!"

"How did you do that?"

"You were amazing!" the girls commented.

I was so excited I would never have to hide my face I might even become popular.

"I think I got bit!" I said "It really hurts!" I added as we ran up stairs to get my mom and dad. We explained the whole story to them as they rushed me to the hospital.

"It was all good in the end" I told my mom after she asked how the sleep over went. I told her about my babyish sleeping bag and she told me that if the girls only cared about the stuff I had like, a plasma screen TV or a babyish sleeping bag I shouldn't hang out with the popular girls at school.

"I don't want to be part of the In Crowd if they just want to be friends with me because of the stuff I have and not caring about me as a person".

I'll make my own In Crowd and hang out with people who like me for who I am. I don't need to be perfect when I am with my true friends.

Mackenzie Fleming
6th Grade

My Fear is a Fantasy, Or Is It?

Challenge is a dragon with a gift in its mouth... Tame the dragon and the gift is yours.

Noela Evans

"This is creepy," whispered Jake.

Jake was walking though a tunnel with his family. An older sister named Marisa, two younger brothers, twins: Ron and Jim, and his mom.

"What's that?" Jake looked to left. A big red pile of dragon scales was right on a tunnel. Suddenly a dragon came out of the tunnel.

"AAAAHHHHH" screamed Jake.

The dragon started talking to him.

"Wake up," it started to sound like his mom, "Wake up sweetie, wake up", it was his mom!

"AAAAHHHHH!" Jake yelled. He was sitting up in his bed.

"Bad dream again?" his mom asked.

"Yep." Jake replied.

"You know I do have a spell that can stop bad dreams."

"I know mom, you told me before, it didn't work."

"Well it only works for bad DREAMS, maybe yours is a nightmare."

"I need to go get my broom license mom."

"Ok." said his mom. He got up and went to the closet to get his clothes. His mom walked out.

Not too much later his younger brothers came into his room.

"Morning Ron, morning Jim." said Jake.

"Morning." said the twins, "So how did you sleep?" asked Jim.

"Not too good Ron." said Jake.

"Helloooo, I'm Jim he's Ron, remember?" said Jim pointing to himself and his brother Ron.

"Right, right." said Jake hurriedly. It was only an hour until his test.

"Off to get my broom license." said Jake.

"We forgot to tell you that Marisa got a new job, it's a..."

"Well I'm off; bye."

"...broom license instructor," said Ron even though Jake had gone out the door. "Oh well I guess we'll tell him when he gets back, where did say he was going again?"

"I forgot, want to put a stink bomb in his pillow?" asked Jim.

"Duh, let's go." said Ron excitedly.

Meanwhile Jake was trying to catch a taxi broom to his class.

"C'mon, I'm going to be late, and I have a new instructor for the test." said Jake impatiently. "Oh there's one. BROOM!!" Jake yelled.

A broom taxi stopped in front of him.

"Grood day sir, where are you want'en to go today?" asked the taxi man.

Jake realized that the bad grammar meant that the taxi man had a bit too much relaxing potion.

"This is going to be fun." thought Jake.

"The Broom Ed. School please." said Jake.

"Right, that learning joint, well hop on." said the taxi man.

Five minutes later, the taxi man stopped right in front of The Broom Ed. School of Virginia.

"Well tis is duh place right?" asked the taxi man.

"Yes it is, here can you accept ten bucks?" asked Jake handing out a ten dollar bill in his hand.

"Yep sure can...by the way me name's Jordan if you sees me again." said Jordan while mounting his broom.

"Bye Jordan!" yelled Jake since he was running toward the school. Jordan took off. Jake ran around the school towards the testing area, where his new broom instructor was turned around talking to someone else.

"I'm here, I'm here!" yelled Jake still a yard away from the broom. The new instructor turned around. It was Marisa.

"What are you doing here?" asked Jake in astonishment.

"Didn't the twins tell you? I got a job here." said Marisa looking confused.

"No, they didn't tell me." admitted Jake.

Marisa looking a bit shocked herself and paused a moment.

"All right I must warn you about two things, ok?" asked Marisa.

"Ok." said Jake.

"Number one, just because I'm your sister doesn't mean I'm going to let you pass. I'm giving you the same treatment as everybody else." said Marisa.

"Ok." said Jake.

"Number two, there are new challenges on the test field. Some students get scared and they run for their moms." said Marisa in a low voice looking a little worried.

"Well are you worried?" asked Marisa after a short pause.

"I...I'm not worr...worried." said Jake in a squeaky voice. Marisa paused to look Jake's written test score that he took the day before. Then she looked up.

"All right, this is how this is going to work." said Marisa. "Our brooms are going to be attached with these hand-cuffs in case you get knocked out." In Marisa's hands were a pair of hand-cuffs, the kind the wizard police use.

"If for any reason you or I get knocked out, you or I can take charge, ok?" asked Marisa as she attached one cuff on one broom and the other cuff on the other broom.

"Go through the orange cones, you need at least an 85 to pass this test.

"Ready…Set…GO!" yelled Marisa.

Jake and Marisa took off. Jake's control was graceful but he bumped into a rock while going. Marisa wrote something on the paper. Jake headed for the first pair of cones and continued the test.

Jake was doing very well until he noticed something at the back of his broom.

"I'm losing straw sis!" yelled Jake.

"Land in that cave. That's where the test ends." said Marisa pointing at a little hole in the ground.

Jake started toward the cave when he noticed an all to familiar red pile of dragon scales. The pile moved and just as Jake had feared, it was a dragon.

"HOLY HORSERADISH!!!" Jake yelled, pointing to the dragon coming straight for Jake and Marisa.

"Hurry Jake, fly toward the cave quickly!" yelled Marisa.

Jake thought for a moment and remembered his dream, he thought to himself, "I am not letting my dream come true." He turned toward the dragon and used the blowtorch attack with his wand.

"BLOWTORCH!!" he yelled and huge strips of fire came out of his wand and hit the dragon. What was odd was that once the fire hit the dragon, the dragon disappeared all together.

"Where did it go?" asked Jake. Shortly after he finished his sentence the last broom straw falls off. Jake and Marisa began to hurtle toward the ground.

"HOLY…!" Jake never finished. He hit the ground and passed out. Marisa did not get hurt as bad. As soon as she recovered she attempted to wake up Jake.

"Jake, Jake wake up." said Marisa. Jake slowly opened his eyes.

"Did I pass?" asked Jake.

Marisa laughed.

"Of course you passed. You destroyed that image of the dragon."

"Image? That wasn't real?" asked Jake.

"No, that was part of the test." said Marisa. "You got a 99.99, you were a little bumpy at the beginning. Congratulations!"

"I PASSED!" yelled Jake. He jumped high happily and yelled again, "I PASSED!"

Jake was so excited, that he ran to the nearest broom store and bought the cheapest broom he could buy.

He rode his beauty home and yelled to his family "I PASSED!"

He walked to his room and laid his head on his pillow. All of a sudden a green gas came out his pillow.

"RONNN, JIMMM!!"

He heard laughter across the hall. Jake opened his window and let all the gas flow go out the window. He laid his head down on his pillow again and fell asleep. Little did he know an all too familiar red pile of scales was outside his window watching him.

Maddy Goshorn
7th Grade

Plane Wreck

You must do the things you think you cannot do.

Eleanor Roosevelt

"You're kidding, right?" my twelve year old cousin Sophie asked as she snatched the basketball right out of my hands and dribbled down the driveway toward the hoop.

"No, I'm serious. I'm afraid of flying," I admitted, ashamed of myself. I wasn't lying. I've never ridden a plane before, and I'm petrified of them. I'm too much of a wimp to even ride the flight simulators at the Aeronautics Center.

I grabbed the ball from Sophie before she was able to throw it into the hoop.

"Evan, you can't be afraid of riding a plane. A, you're fourteen years old; and B, only one out of every zillion planes crashes." Sophie teased. She kicked me in the shin and caught the ball when I dropped it in pain.

"Freak," I said, wishing that I could think of a better comeback through all of my humiliation. I rubbed my shin in pain as she dunked the basketball into the basket and stuck her tongue out at me.

"Oh, ouch, that hurt." Sophie mocked, "I can't believe how good you are at hurting my feelings." She took the ball again and sat on it, swaying back and forth.

"C'mon, you've been watching way too much *Lost.* We're not going to end up on some island in the middle of nowhere."

I walked over to her and kicked the ball out from under her. Sophie landed hard on the pavement.

"How're you going to get to Grandma Cameron's if you can't ride a plane? It's a long walk from here to Illinois," she said.

I sat down on the ball next to where Sophie sat on the pavement, pulling her hair back into a ponytail.

"I'm going to have to ride the plane anyway, so I might as well stop complaining," I said.

Sophie grinned mischievously, "Worrywart."

***

Okay, just between you and me, the day I would be getting on the plane arrived too quickly. It was supposed to be four days away, but instead it felt like one and a half. So there I was, standing in the airport terminal, holding my passport, ticket and backpack, looking like a complete idiot. I had no clue what to do (in reality, there were little arrows and signs all over the place and I knew exactly where I was supposed to go I was just afraid) and to make me feel even more stupid, I had know-it-all Sophie standing right next to me, telling me what to do.

"Evan. The plane leaves in twenty minutes. Don't you think we should actually get on the plane before then?" Sophie asked sarcastically, bouncing in her squeaky sandals. That girl's got guts to be this excited about a plane trip!

"Couldn't we just take a train?" I pleaded. She rolled her eyes, and not saying a word, yanked me over to the gate that led out to the plane. I reluctantly followed, yearning for the plane to have some fateful breakdown before we even got on it.

We walked up into the plane and found our seats. I closed my eyes tight and gripped the armrests as I sat down. Sophie already had a Green Day song blaring on her CD-Walkman and was looking at pictures of Johnny Depp.

The plane started down the runway a few minutes later. It wasn't long before we were in the air. Of course, by then, I was praying to God that we wouldn't crash.

"Would you like something to drink?" a flight attendant asked loudly in my ear. I opened my eyes with a start. "Water helps if you're afraid of flying," she offered.

"Um, no thank you," I said, completely mortified that even Miss Flight Attendant knew I was a wimp. She nodded and walked away, pushing her cart down the aisle and stopping at the teenage couple in the next row that wouldn't stop giving each other goo-goo eyes.

I rested my head up against the back of my seat again. Moments later I felt a huge jolt and opened my eyes.

"What happened?" I asked Sophie hastily, panicking.

She shook her head, sweating, her magazine and music now lying on the floor beneath her feet.

"The pilot just came on a second ago. Didn't you hear?" She was almost in tears. "One of the engines just fell off!"

"What?" I asked loudly. I noticed out of the corner of my eye that the other passengers were crying and shouting – except for one of them, a pretty astute looking guy, who was sitting calmly in his seat sipping what I assumed was a mimosa.

"We're crashing, idiot!" she yelled at me. She looked out the window and paused momentarily, her eyes widening in fear. "Is that water?"

"Water? We're not supposed to be flying over water!" I cried out, thinking what to do. The pilot started talking over the intercom again, but I was so scared I could barely tell what he was saying.

I couldn't believe it. After all the time that everyone had told me that we wouldn't crash – couldn't crash, even – it was happening. We should have taken the train. Gas masks popped out from the ceiling. As I went to grab mine, Sophie looked at me and started to shake me.

"Evan!" she called out, shaking me with all her might. Why was she shaking me? "Evan!" she said again, "We're there!"

"Get your gas mask on, Sophie!" I said as I pushed her off of me. I went to grab my gas mask, but it was gone and the plane was on the ground. People were piling off, grabbing their bags and talking loudly.

"What?" I murmured, looking up at Sophie, who was now standing in the aisle. "What's going on?" I asked.

"You were dreaming, Evan. I've been trying to wake you up for the past five minutes. Gosh, you're a heavy sleeper."

Timothy Gotimer
8th Grade

The Taco Troops

Great opportunities to help others seldom come, but small ones surround us every day.

Sally Koch

"Bum-Bum-Bada-Bum" sang Josie.

Josie was on her way back from school. She had to walk 15 miles to and from school. She was on her 13th mile and she traumatically tripped on an empty bottle of hot sauce lying in the middle of the dirt path. Josie went down and hit the ground with a loud "thud."

"HELP ME. SOMEBODY HELP!!" Josie cried.

The nearest house was a mile away but it was Mr. Finderry's house and Josie had never quite liked him. Oh well, she had to see if she could actually walk first.

As soon as Josie got herself together she tried to take a measly little step but she just fell again! So, Josie just stayed on the ground, writing in the dirt with a stick she had found.

After and hour (which seemed like forever and a year), Josie spotted something coming down the winding dirt path. She couldn't make out exactly what the figure was but she could see the out line of it. *What was it?* It was the oddest of shapes. As the figures approached Josie saw several other shapes following the largest figure.

As the tribe came closer Josie backed away, stick in hand ready to fight and protect herself from whatever was coming her way. They came closer and as they did Josie could see that they were wearing large, round, and vibrant colored on their heads. *Were they hats?* Yes but they were not just any average Joe regular hats, they were sombreros. The mysterious figures were not just any mysterious figures; they were Mexican Hat Dancing, Sombrero wearing, hot sauce eating mysterious figures.

When the figures were closer to her than two peas in a pod, Josie got the courage from somewhere inside of her to try to stand up. She inched her way up till she was on her feet then she instantly fell back down to the ground. Her ankle just hurt so badly.

When Josie looked up she saw two eyes staring her straight in the face. She closed her eyes with shock and fright.

Was she dreaming?

No she couldn't be, because she felt the pain throbbing in her ankle. She looked up again and the creature and her met eyes.

"Hola I'm Cackaback and these are my fellow taco troops. I'd tell you their names but they are far too long and confusing, but any way, we are here to help."

"W-h-a-t-t?" Josie stammered.

"Oh, it is quite all right, we get this a lot." Cackaback said.

"Um ... what are you talking about?" Josie asked as she sat up.

"Well you are speechless because of our great beauty right?" spoke Cackaback. "No need to answer because we will do the Mexican Hat Dance for you. Ready Boys?"

Duh-da-da-da-duh-da ... sang the old radio while the tacos followed along with Cackaback.

After the troops little rendition, Cackaback

hushed the tacos then started to speak to Josie. 'Child my troops and I have an offering for you. We will take you home on one condition."

"Ok Sir, what is it?" Josie asked.

"We want hot sauce." Cackaback replied.

"Um, ok" Josie answered.

After that Josie found herself floating in midair then landing peacefully into the arms of the taco troops. As they marched in rhythm with one another, Josie daydreamed then eventually dozed off into a peaceful sleep.

When they arrived at Josie's house, the troops gently placed Josie on her front porch. Then Cackaback woke her up.

"Josie darling, wake up you are home. Also do not forget our hot sauce."

"Thank you so much for taking me home Cackaback, and you too, taco troops" Josie said as she woke up.

"You are very welcome." They all replied in unison.

"Well I would go get you the hot sauce but I can't still can't walk." Josie said.

"Oh, about that, you actually can because while you were sleeping, we cured you with some old Mexican Remedies." Cackaback informed her.

"Thank you very much." Josie said.

"Our pleasure." they all said together."

“Well, I guess I'll go get the hot sauce now" Josie said.

A few moments later Josie came out the door with hot sauce.

"Sorry guys, we only had three bottles and 5 little packets from Taco Bell" Josie told them.

"Oh, it is quite alright." Cackaback said.

"Thank you so much for helping me, I really appreciate it." Josie said as she hugged Cackaback and blew a kiss to the troops.

"It was our pleasure and we will miss you very much." Cackaback said as tears welled in his eyes.

Then faster then the fastest cheetah, the troops and Cackaback were gone.

"Josie get out of bed, you're going to be late for school"

Were am I? The troops are gone and I'm in bed. What happened?

Josie's mother appeared in her doorway with a laundry basket resting on her right hip and her hand on the other.

"Josie I really mean it. I've told you to get up three times now."

"Mom, my ankle.... And the tacos.... The hot sauce.... Where is Cackaback?"

"Honey I don't know what you're talking about, you were probably just dreaming."

"If you're so upset about the tacos or whatever I guess we can go to taco bell tonight for dinner. Now get a move on." Josie's mom said as she walked down the hallway.

As Josie got up out of bed, she could see in the window through the corner of her eye, Cackaback and the troops marching down the road.

Shannon Graney
6th Grade

Archie Smith: Boy Wonder

No matter how many times you save the world, it always manages to get back in jeopardy again.

Mr. Incredible

Archie Smith walked sleepily up to the stairs to his bedroom. He turned on the lights, yawning. He brushed his teeth and got ready for bed. He had spent all night starting and finishing a project that was due the next day.

"Why didn't you start it two weeks ago when you had the chance?" Archie's mom had said.

Archie climbed into his bed and turned off the lights. He quickly fell fast asleep. There is something you do not know about Archie, but I will get into that later on in the story. Now on with the story.

Brinng Brinng went his bedroom phone.

The voice on the other line said, "Archie Smith Boy Wonder we need your help!" *Weeee Oooh Weee Oooh.* The sounds of police cars went roaring past his bedroom widow. He quickly changed and flew out the window. It was 2:00 in the morning so he could not help yawning.

He flew to a police officer and said, "What's going on?"

The police officer replied, "There has been a robbery at the town bank!"

Archie quickly flew to the bank. He was still tired but he knew that he had to do his job. He tiptoed into the bank and heard a man mumbling something.

“Stupid police officers think they are so smart waiting outside. I am not about to waltz right out the front door and get caught.”

“No, catching you is my job,” said Archie.

The robber turned around in shock. In a second the robber was running to the back door not worrying about the alarms he had set of. He ran fast but not as fast as Archie. By the time the robber got to the door Archie was already standing there with a pair of handcuffs. Archie posed for a few pictures and was on his way.

Five minutes later Archie’s cell phone rang “Archie Smith Boy Wonder, we need your help! Dr. Carton has escaped from the town jail and none of our sensors are picking up any movement in the town.”

Archie rudely hung up the phone and went to his sensors.

“He was right!” Archie said aloud.

The sensors were not picking up anything. Archie even tried changing the batteries! He ran his lamp so he could see a little better, but it would not turn on, and neither would his bathroom light.

“This must have something to do with Dr. Carton,” he mumbled.

All of the sudden the sensors started beeping and a white dot (the symbol that represent villains) came up from the ground. Archie stopped and stared at the dot that was coming towards him. It was getting closer and then disappeared. Archie went down the stairs slowly and steadily listening to any sound he could pick up. He cautiously opened the front door and saw.... nothing not even a star in the sky.

He was very confused. Then his sensor watch started beeping rapidly. Someone was coming. It quickly vanished again. All of the sudden Archie fell to the ground and drifted off into a deep sleep.

He awoke in a dark room that appeared to be underground. He tried to move his arms but they were chained to a wall, as were his feet. Then Archie saw a tall dark figure approach in the dark room. It was not Dr. Carton or any other person.

The shadow approached. Archie tried to turn his head so he could see his watch and in bright yellow letters were the words, “Dr. Carton has been caught.” Archie started breathing harder and harder and sweat poured down his face. His heart stopped beating and all he could hear was the footsteps of the figure and the water dripping from the walls.

Beep beep beep went the sound of Archie’s alarm clock. He got dressed to go to school. The thing that you have been dying to know about Archie is that he is a good dreamer.

Jesseca Hoff
6th Grade

The Diary of Laura Banks: Hurricane Katrina Victim

The world is full of suffering, it is also full of the overcoming of it.
Helen Keller

Dear Diary,

Today was the most horrifying experience of my life. Water came towards me rapidly, almost as if it was opening its mouth to roar like a lion. I watched people helplessly sinking into the water and not coming back up. I watched from my rooftop and saw the whole New Orleans flooded in water. My parents left the house before it all happened so now I sit here waiting and hoping. Waiting for someone, anyone, to come and rescue me from this nightmare, and hoping my parents are alive. It is impossible for me to sleep because the thoughts and images of what happened today still float around in my mind and because I am in need of something to eat and drink.

Dear Diary,

Today human bodies floated lifelessly in the water with shock still on their faces. I watched people on rooftops drop of dehydration since we should not drink the floodwater because it was contaminated when the levees burst yesterday. The water is now brown and green. My only hope right now is that someone rescues me soon before I die of dehydration and starvation.

Dear Diary,

I was found today! Two rescuers paddled to my house and told me to climb down from my roof. We have now been paddling for what seems like days and my stomach is growling louder than ever. As we pushed dead bodies out of our way I recognized many faces. As tears stream down my face I saw a man paddling out of a house holding what seemed to be a television. I asked one of my rescuers what the man was doing and he replied in one word "looting."

Dear Diary,

We have paddled out of New Orleans to dry land! We boarded a plane with many other passengers with looks of sorrow on their faces. The plane took us to the Superdome in Texas. It looks like a billion people are inside there. We are given a small amount of food and water! I ate mine sparingly, just in case we run out. I also have looked around for my parents but have not succeeded yet.

Dear Diary,

Today the toilets in the bathroom overflowed so we are no longer able to use them. Each day we are given less food and each day people die of diseases spread around the Superdome. Still no luck finding my parents. I long to go back to my house but sadly there is nothing to go back to.

Dear Diary,

I have found my dad! Sadly my mother is not alive anymore. She was swept away in the flow of the water so fast that my father could not reach her before she drowned. I shed many tears that day -- some tears of joy for finding my dad but mostly tears of sorrow for my mother's lost life. I have one wish right now and that is that this tragic event never happened. I wish this because so many lives were lost. So many that I think someone from everyplace in the world is mourning over the lost lives of loved ones. But lucky for me I still have someone.

Jesseca Hoff
6th Grade

I Believe

The thing always happens that you really believe in; and the belief in a thing makes it happen.

Frank Lloyd Wright

Everything happened on a street name I will never forget: Tovito Dr. It was located in a small neighborhood called Mantua. My family and I had just moved from Germany, and we were living at our Grandma's house. She lived in America while her daughter, my mom, and her family lived in Germany.

I was outside one relaxing spring day, in July of the year 1998. I was only six years old and couldn't speak English that well. Yet, once we met, that, and nothing else, seemed to matter.

His name was Joe Milan. We met at the park one day, and I decided to walk home with him. I was blown away once we got to his house, because it was right across the street from my grandma's! It was really sweet meeting him, since I had no friends since our "big day", the move from Germany.

He wasn't really the biggest kid, but he wasn't the smallest either, he was average. Joe was never really mean or nasty or crude. He was willing to sacrifice if he had to. He was African American. He wore glasses and had a small afro for a haircut. He was never a good athlete, but still sporty guy. Now when I say he wasn't a good athlete, don't take it as if he were scrawny, because he wasn't. And when I say "sporty", I mean he liked sports. He did normal things just like any other guy.

We were best friends; we were also each others worst friends. We were each other's only friend. He was my first friend in America, but then again he was also the first kid in America. We did everything together. If he had a baseball game, or I had a basketball game, the other would be the loudest one cheering him on. I would always eat dinner at his house. Then after dinner we would walk across the street and he'd sleep over at my house. We had so much fun.

The fun got better when we played with boxer. He was my Belgian shepherd. He was a good boy, and a great companion. Even when he went for a swim in the creek behind my grandma's house, and smelled like a skunk. Yet, we still played with him.

We would laugh so much when boxer licked our ears. We'd feel this wet, gooey, slime all over our ears. It would take us a couple of minutes and many tissues to get all the spit out of our ears. The best part about his licking was the sound. All we'd hear would be what sounded like a drum, beating away at our eardrums. The sound would travel farther into our heads, and wrap like a snake around our minds. It was the weirdest sensation, yet the sweetest part.

Then Joe's whole family had a "big day." We had overheard his mom and dad talking about the "big day," but we never really paid attention to it. Then one day, I went over to his house to see if he could play 'water guns' with me.

I rang the bell and waited and waited and waited. I waited for fifteen minutes, which seemed like an hour to me, and then left. I figured he was out doing errands with his mom. The same thing happened for the next week; I would go over to his house, ring the bell, wait, then give up. I asked my mom what was going on. She said Joe's family had moved. I was so shocked and felt terrible. Luckily, my mom knew where they had moved and had Joe's phone number. They lived only ten minutes away in a townhouse. So we were still best friends. We just didn't get to see each other as much. A couple of months went on like that. Although we lived farther apart, we still had tons of fun. But as usual, right when we were at the peak of our friendship, it was time for another of Joe's "big days."

This time he lived thirty five minutes away. We only saw each other twice a month. Joe and I were living farther and farther apart. This was bad, really bad. I felt as if a thin rope with a time bomb attached to it, connected us. And that time bomb was about to blow.

The worst part was that he moved again. This time my mom didn't know where he was. I seemed to forget him. I lived my life, made new friends and hung out with other kids. Two years passed, and then it happened. I was walking home with a friend. We were we were just passing my house, when a car came speeding by. It created such a rush of air that my friend fell over. The car came to a screeching halt and out jumped Joe.

He had been living twenty minutes away the whole two years. We became best friends again. We hung out at the mall near our house. We played videogames, we played football, we rode bikes, and we were spending time together again. The dynamic duo was back in black. It was too good to be true and I knew it. After all the times he had moved, it was finally my turn. I moved away from Fairfax County, to Ashburn. After a month of living in Loudon County, I called him, but no one answered.

That was two years ago. We used to be so close. Now I don't even know if he lives in this state. I don't know his phone number or his address. I guess this is what it means to grow up. The whole time I knew him, even all the fights, where the best times I have ever had with a friend. Who knows, maybe someday years from now, I will be walking along the street when a car comes screeching to a halt. I believe it will. I do believe.

Calvin B. Hollenhorst
7th Grade

A Search for Disaster

Man cannot discover new oceans unless he has the courage to lose sight of the shore.

Andre Gide

It was a warm evening when Chris' plane landed at Honolulu International Airport. As he stepped out of the plane he was greeted by girls in grass skirts who said "Aloha", and put leis around his neck. Chris wished he could stay longer, but this was not a pleasure trip. Chris was a diver from EQP (Earthquake Prediction) International. People along the coast of Maunalua Bay, had recently reported some rumbling and Chris had been sent to check it out.

Chris would spend most of this trip alone on a small company boat, The Monarch. Chris pulled up to the dock and saw the boat in the bay. It was 20 feet long with plenty of space for his diving gear, and various tools for measuring plate movement. Under the deck was a small diving sub which Chris nicknamed Clownfish. It could be dropped into the ocean through a hatch on the bottom of the vessel. The sub had an airlock that allowed Chris to dive outside of the mini-sub, investigate what he needed to, then get back in the sub and continue his search for earthquakes.

After loading supplies and making checks on the

boat and Clownfish, Chris finally got on the water. Cruising along, Chris stole glances at his laptop to make sure he was on course.

Around noon Chris got to his first dive sight. His seismograph in the cockpit didn't register any tectonic movement, but he would have to wait until he put one on the bottom of the ocean before he really knew what was happening with the earth's plates here. Chris sent his coordinates to the EQP base in Panhala, Hawaii so if something happened, someone would know his location. He loaded his diving gear, and a seismograph into Clownfish, and then climbed in himself.

As Chris closed the hatch he heard a terrible scraping sound. He looked at the hinges on the door and saw the problem. The edge of the hatch had bent not allowing it to close properly. Chris forced it closed, glad that awful sound was only a small problem.

Chris climbed into the seat in front of a control panel, loaded with buttons, levers, and gauges. He pulled the overhead lever that deployed Clownfish from its holding area and let it out into the Hawaiian waters. The mini-sub began to descend, slowly at first, but gradually speeding up as it sunk deeper into the dark water of Maunalua Bay. Chris switched on strobe lights to see through the murky, deep-sea water. When he got close to the bottom, he fired the engine, and cruised through the deep very slowly. Even though Chris' submarine was capable of going very fast, he wanted to be sure not to miss anything that could mean a possible earthquake.

Chris maneuvered Clownfish over the terrain of the Pacific Plate until he saw where he could place the seismograph. Then he put on his diving gear, grabbed the seismograph, and entered the airlock. Once he was sure the door behind him was sealed, Chris pushed a button and opened the door to the sea world.

Instantly the airlock flooded with water, and Chris, alone, drifted out into the bay.

As Chris took in his surroundings he noticed a shark chasing a school of fish and made a note to stay out of its way. He swam over to a sandy gap just behind a rock and placed the seismograph there, all the while watching out for the shark. After everything was set correctly, Chris swam back toward Clownfish. When he got to the airlock he opened it and then climbed inside. Once inside, Chris took one last look to assure the shark wasn't following him, pressed a button and the flooded airlock began to drain. After all the water was pumped out, Chris removed his diving gear, and climbed into the cockpit. He began to pilot Clownfish toward the surface of the bay.

Chris spent the rest of the day placing 22 more seismographs in various, preplanned locations around Maunalua Bay. No real problems occurred with these missions, the only incident being a barracuda lurking where Chris was going to place the seismograph. Chris enjoyed the sea life. A few of his dives were into lively coral reefs with brightly colored fish, and once even saw a distant pod of humpback whales.

Chris spent the next day going to different sites, collecting rock samples, and testing them for signs that they had been moved or shaken. His last mission of the day was in a long narrow canyon, only ten feet wide. Chris slowed down to maneuver his way through the constricted space and glanced at his GPS.

When he got deep in the ravine, Chris shifted himself to the controls of Clownfish's collector. As he extended it, Chris felt a sudden wrench forward, followed by a violent jolt and Clownfish was thrown against the canyon wall. Dazed it took Chris a moment to realize what was happening. The earthquake he had been looking for was going on beneath him, and he was trapped a mile inside a narrow underwater gorge! He jumped to action. Chris turned Clownfish around and pushed her to full throttle. He hadn't gone 50 feet when lava exploded out of the canyon wall! The vicious earthquake had torn open Earth's crust and allowed molten rock to come up from the mantle!

As Chris pushed Clownfish to maximum speed, rocks and pieces of the canyon collapsed onto the mini-sub. As he sped through the narrow space between the rock walls, Chris noticed they were caving in! More lava explosions were all around him. Just when he thought the rocks would crush him, he saw the end of the gorge, but it was closing fast. Chris tried to make his mini-sub go faster but it refused. Clownfish got closer to the rapidly closing end of the canyon; the space was ten feet wide, then nine, eight, seven. Chris realized he wasn't going to make it! *"This is the end"* he thought. He tried to stop, but he was going too fast. The entrance closed. Clownfish was about to smash into the closed canyon at full speed, when suddenly there was a huge explosion and the entrance was miraculously blasted open. Clownfish sped through the fiery outburst into the open water.

With his heart pounding, Chris accelerated toward The Monarch. After docking Clownfish, he ran to the deck of his vessel and called EQP to report his crisis. They dispatched a crew to pick him up.

It was not easy to drive The Monarch back to the dock. The Earthquake had made the bay extremely rough, and the boat was rocking crazily. When he finally got back, Chris shared his discovery with the National Weather Service. After that he decided to join a Luau along the beach. His job was done. He had found the earthquake and now he could relax and enjoy the girls in grass skirts who said "Aloha" and put leis around his neck.

Joseph Kane
Grade 7

Snow Dance

School's a weird thing. I'm not sure it works.

Johnny Depp

James and Robert stared blankly out the window. It was already December, and there was no snow yet. It was the most disgusting thing they had ever seen.

"*Man*, I wish it would snow," James slumped pathetically.

"I know," Robert cradled his head in his hands. "I can't stand it. It's so... not snowy outside."

Robert could almost hear James's brainstorming juices sloshing around in his head.

"Hey," James shouted suddenly, "a kid at my school said that if you throw ice cubes out your bedroom window, it'll snow the next morning."

"And a kid at *my* school said that if you wear your pajamas inside out, there'll be snow flurries," Robert was getting caught up in James's plot, "and you make up a 'snow dance' for extra good luck."

"It couldn't hurt to try it," James shrugged.

As you could probably tell, the two brothers were very superstitious boys.

Robert ran upstairs with a clump of freezing, frosty ice from the ice maker in a large mug.

Opening the window, James shouted, "Let 'er rip!"

Robert dumped the ice cubes out the window, and at last they heard a 'thump' as the ice hit the ground.

"Step one, complete!" James laughed and gave his brother a high five.

When James and Robert got ready for bed, they wore their pajamas, socks, and even underwear inside out (this was how desperate they were). Cranking the volume up on the stereo, Robert put in his favorite Christmas CD in the player.

Oh, the weather outside is frightful,
And the fire is so delightful,
And since we've no place to go,
Let it snow, let it snow, let it snow.

As the music blared throughout the house, James and Robert ridiculously boogied to the liveliness of the song. James shimmied. Robert waltzed. They were a pair of dancing fools. But they didn't care. All they cared about was snow.

The next morning, the two brothers woke to a horrific surprise. It was just as bare as it was the last night. Not a single snowflake had fallen from the sky.

"Aw, man," James whined.

"Don't worry," Robert patted James's shoulder sympathetically. "Let's try it again tonight. Maybe it'll work then."

James felt a little better.

That night, they dropped a bucket-full of ice out their window, turned their pajamas inside out, and danced their silly snow dance—just as they had done the night before.

Oh, the fire is slowly dying,
And, my dear, we're still good bye-ing,

But as long as you love me so,
Let it snow, let it snow, let it snow.

•

As soon as day broke, James and Robert bolted out of bed and to the window. They slumped immediately when they saw what was outside--nothing. The grass was still green, and the trees as dry and bare as a piece of toast with no butter or jelly.

That night, James and Robert continued their routine for snow, but, this time, without the confidence that they had the previous nights.

The next morning, there was still no snow.

Each and every evening, the boys' hopes began to drop tremendously. They realized that no matter how much ice they threw out the window, no matter how many times they wore their pajamas inside out, and no matter how gracefully they danced, there wouldn't be any snow.

One night, James and Robert flopped glumly into bed. They didn't even try to do their ritual. Their dreams of a white Christmas were shattered.

"Let's face it, Rob," James said, "The kids at school must have been lying or something."

"Yeah, it was all just a waste of time." Robert covered his head with his blankets.

The next morning, as the boys got ready for school, James looked out the window. He was awoken at once by the amazing sight.

"Robert! Look outside! Look outside!"

The whole world was draped in a blanket of blinding white snow, with tiny flakes of frost falling from the heavens. At least three feet of snow covered the ground.

"Woah," Robert admired the view, his eyes widening, "it's pitch white outside!"

"Yeah," James laughed. "Guess our snow dance worked after all!"

The two brothers raced outside with their sled, ready to have amazing and marvelous adventures in the snow.

Brian Marshall Loy
7th Grade

Another Place Another Time

Where children are, there is the golden age.

Novalis

"This story begins hundreds of years ago when the West was an ocean and not a desert," said Niko's Dad.

"Your ancestor, Captain Nicholas, sailed the toughest and most dangerous seas. One night he was called to cross the far west ocean to find a missing man that feel off a cruise ship. Your ancestor accepted the mission. He set off the next day, and for the next week he looked for the man but never found him. On the 13th day your ancestor finally aborted the mission because a thunderstorm was brewing. On his way back he heard a desperate cry for help. He turned to the way the voice was. The closer your ancestor got to the sound the worse the thunderstorm became. After a few minutes of searching the captain spotted a large castle in the distance. The voice of man became clearer and clearer as they neared the castle. At this time the storm was making 50-foot waves and 200 mile per hour winds. The boat was about 200 meters from land when a lightning bolt struck the hull. When the boat was sinking he looked at the castle one last time and he wrote one last sentence in his journal." Niko's dad got up and took a book from the shelf and sat down.

These are the final words he wrote. "As my ship sinks and my crew screams I write my final words, the man I once heard in the water is gone, but I hope that someone finds this diary and looks for the castle that I once saw."

Niko's dad paused and then turned the page. He withdrew an envelope and opened it.

"Niko," his dad said. "This is the map that your ancestor drew when he was sailing. Niko, when every boy and girl becomes 14, their parents tell then the story of the castle. If you want to go to the castle you will be very surprised at what you find there. When I was your age I went to the same place and so did you ancestors for hundreds of years."

"Dad, I've only been as far as the market," said Niko. "I don't even know where to go."

"You'll just have to use the map. I used the exact same map when I was 14."

"All right dad, I'll head out tomorrow."

The next morning Niko left town to search for the castle. On the 13th day, Niko saw the figure of a tall building. He walked for about another mile and came across an odd go-cart machine. The weird thing about this go-cart was that it was made out of wood and it was on tracks. Niko walked up to it. Two other kids were sitting in it.

"Hey," Niko shouted. "What are you two doing in this machine?"

"Well, we're waiting for a third person to ride to the Ultimate Kid Paradise."

The boy that replied was black, a sort of Native American boy.

"Hop in," the second boy said.

Niko jumped into the go-cart type machine. He looked around at it. It was a triangle box that has a sail sticking up from the middle.

"By the way," the native boy said. "I'm Stephen and to my right is Travis."

"How did you two get here?" Niko asked.

"Let's get movin' and we'll explain on the way," said Stephen.

He yanked a rope and the sail came rolling down. Travis took a bar and pushed it forward, and the device started moving.

"What's your name?" asked Travis.

"Oh, my name is Niko. So how did you two get here?" asked Niko.

"After finding America my ancestor decided to stay here instead of going back to Africa."

"My parents died a while back so I've been on my own," replied Travis. Don't pay much attention to that. How did you find this place, Niko?"

"One of my forefathers sailed to this place when it was an ocean and drew a map of this place. What is the Ultimate Kid Paradise?"

"It is the best place in the world," exclaimed Travis. "They have the best books, the best food, and the best playgrounds."

"Don't forget Travis, there are no adults to tell us what to do!"

Creeeeeeeeek, the cart was starting to slow down.

"Hey, we're here," said Stephen.

Niko looked over the sail and saw thousands of kids doing whatever they wanted. Some were playing on a jungle gym, some were reading, and others just seemed to be happy.

"Come on Niko I want you to meet some kids," said Travis. "Niko, this is Jeff, he's like the main kid leader. Don't be afraid of him, though, he's real nice. Jeff this is Niko, he's new."

"Hi, Niko," said Jeff. "If there's anything you need just come to me."

"Alright," Niko replied.

"Dinners about to begin and I'm starving," said Stephen.

“Kids, today we have a new member to our kid paradise,” Jeff announced. “Niko, come up here and introduce yourself to all the other kids.”

Niko hurried up to the stage.

“Hi everybody and my name is Niko.”

“Niko, why don’t you tell us something special about yourself.”

“Alright, I’m pretty talented at…”

“Sorry to interrupt Niko, but we got an army of adults heading this way,” said the messenger boy.

“Go tell the boys to start up the force field and that I will be up there once everyone is in the safe hanger,” said Jeff. “Niko, I heard you were a great engineer, can you go up to the tower and see if the kids need any help?”

“Sure, replied Niko.

When Niko got there the kids had just turned the field on the adults were banging into it. When Jeff arrived one of the kids told him that the field wasn’t going to hold much longer.

“Wait, Jeff, I can do something, watch this,” said Niko. Niko studied the control circuit for a moment, then took a screwdriver from his pocket and started changing the position of some wires.

“What did you do?” asked Jeff.

“I changed the field so that it’s a confusion force field.”

Sure enough, the adults immediately began arguing amongst themselves and appeared to forget that they were trying to enter the Paradise. When Niko got to the bottom of the tower everyone was waiting for him. Then they all cheered for him.

“Niko, you saved our home and paradise, you are a hero from this day on,” said Jeff. “Now, let’s finish our celebration.”

Everyone sat down at their seats and started the feast. Every time the kids got a chance they congratulated him.

“Well, everybody this has been the best day of my life but it’s time for this day to end,” said Niko. Niko climbed into the go-cart machine and waved goodbye.

“Don’t forget Niko, come back anytime you want,” shouted Jeff.

Niko looked back at the building and saw that it wasn’t a building; it was a castle, the same one his ancestor saw. Niko would go back anytime he wanted, especially if he needed an answer. Because if there was an answer, he would find it there.

Ryan Nau
7th Grade

The Ice Cave

Advice is like snow; the softer it falls, the longer it dwells upon, and the deeper it sinks into, the mind.

Samuel Taylor Coleridge

It was a chilly day in late autumn at the foot of the Equina Glacier in the Himalayas. Mark, a young scientist at the Snow Leopard Conservation Station, was just about to step outside into the misty morning with his two loyal Bernese mountain dogs when he heard footsteps behind him.

"Going somewhere?"

Mark turned around to face the person who had spoken. She was Lindsay, a fellow researcher and his best friend.

"Well, Wes said a couple days ago that he found snow leopard tracks at the Kundja Pass, and I want to go check it out. It won't take me long."

"I remember that," said Lindsay, "But I also recall that when Wes and the others left for supplies this morning, he told us to stay put, and I quote, 'It can be dangerous to go out onto the glacier alone.'"

"I'm not going out alone. Blizzard and Hunter are coming with me. I'll be fine," argued Mark.

"I don't think it's wise..." Lindsay began to protest, but by then Mark had gathered up his pack of equipment and gone out the door.

Four hours later, Mark and the dogs were still up on Kundja Pass, unsuccessful in their search for leopard tracks. When Mark saw dark heavy clouds gathering in the sky, he decided to call it quits, but suddenly the dogs bounded through the snow, vanishing into the mist.

Mark called their names, racing toward the sound of their responding barks. When he found them again, he was standing in front of a gaping hole in the wall of a cliff.

The dogs paced back and forth, clearly nervous about something, but Mark ignored them. After switching on the flashlight he had brought in his pack, he stepped forward into the first giant chamber of the cave. Long twisted icicles hung from the ceiling, forming bizarre, beautiful shapes. The floor was solid ice with a bit of snow on top, just enough to keep Mark from slipping when he walked on it.

"Come on, guys! What're you waiting for?" Mark called to his dogs, who still stood at the cave's entrance. After hesitating a moment, Hunter trotted forward and Blizzard soon followed.

"This is amazing!" breathed Mark, staring in wonder at the beautiful rock and ice formations in the cave.

When he came to a dark, narrow tunnel, Mark headed straight inside, eager to explore this new place.

The flashlight cast long, eerie shadows on the ice walls in the dark. As he and the dogs walked through the tunnel, Mark noticed a faint cracking sound beneath his feet. However, he paid it no mind, moving on through the cave with wide eyes.

They walked on and on through the seemingly endless tunnel. When Mark finally began to tire, he turned and looked behind him.

"Gosh, I wonder if I can get back now?" he wondered.

He turned the other way, staring into the darkness before him. About five yards away, he could make out two small black shapes on the cave floor. He shone his flashlight on them, and the bright light revealed two fluffy snow leopard cubs.

"Just look at that, guys!" whispered Mark to the dogs.

Hunter bared his teeth and started to growl deeply in his throat. Whimpering softly, Blizzard just pawed the ground.

The cubs were greatly alarmed at the sight of three large, unfamiliar creatures in their cave, so they began to yowl at the top of their lungs. Mark began to laugh at the sound of their loud crying, but the dogs grew more restless.

Soon two sapphire blue eyes appeared in the shadows, glaring at the intruders. Mark heard a long, low snarl. Now *he* was afraid, and he backed a few feet.

Then a massive snow leopard burst from the darkness. She must have been twice the size of a normal leopard, and she was determined to protect her cubs! She leaped at Mark, screaming with fury.

Mark fell backwards with the cat on top of him. Then, with a loud CRAACCK! the ice gave way beneath him, and he and Hunter plunged into a deep black pit. The leopard jumped clear of the cracking ice, and with her cubs she vanished into the darkness.

Blizzard peered into the pit and barked. She was relieved when Hunter answered her. When the two had fallen, the dog landed on top, so he had no injuries. Immediately Hunter noticed that his master was not moving, so the dog tried to wake him. He laid a paw on Mark's chest. Nothing happened. He even jumped on top of Mark. To his dismay, none of his various attempts proved successful.

Knowing Mark was injured, Blizzard crept slowly through the dark tunnel, gradually making her way to the cave's front chamber and outside. The wind howled treacherously, whirling millions of snowflakes through the air. The air grew colder, and the snow grew deeper, but Blizzard pressed on. She would not leave her master to die in the freezing temperatures.

Back at the Snow Leopard Conservation Station, Lindsay was pacing in the dining room. Mark was somewhere out in the blizzard, but she could do nothing.

By late evening, she heard the front door slam. The other researchers stepped in, covered with snow.

"Whew! That's some weather!" exclaimed Wes, the conservation team leader. "The truck could hardly get through the snow even with the plow on. Hey, where's Mark?"

"I don't know," Lindsay answered glumly. "He left this morning and never came back."

Wes grunted. "He never was one much for followin' orders."

Suddenly, the researchers heard barking at the door. Wes opened it, and Blizzard burst in, her silky black fur turned white with the snow. She was shivering with cold, but she was not ready to rest yet.

She continued barking at the researchers, soon running outside again.

"Maybe she knows where Mark is," said Lindsay.

Hearing Mark's name, Blizzard grew more excited. She barked even louder.

"All right!" Wes hollered, deciding to follow the dog. "Everyone, get in the truck, now!"

The team piled into the truck, and with Blizzard leading the way, the truck slowly plowed through the snow up to the Kundja Pass. When Blizzard stopped in front of the ice cave, everyone ran out of the truck with packs of equipment.

Blizzard led them through the tunnel to the pit where Mark and Hunter had fallen, and Lindsay took up three harnesses-one for herself, two for Mark and Hunter. Then she was lowered into the pit, where she fitted Mark and the dog with harnesses. Because

Hunter had kept his master warm during the long wait, he had saved Mark's life. As soon as the three were hoisted back up, Mark was rushed to the station for medical attention.

Once he had made a full recovery, Mark and his friends set up a hidden camera in the ice cave. The team grew famous for the discovery of the ice cave and for the incredible footage of a mother snow leopard and her cubs. After his accident, Mark became a wiser man, always taking care to follow the sound advice of others.

Sarah Naylor
7th Grade

Friendship and Hershey Bars

Dogs are miracles with paws.

Susan Ariel Rainbow Kennedy

It was a bitter cold night. A full moon shone as the wind howled through the dark alleys. Shadows rose, looming above silvery trashcans and dark corners, swallowing everything in sight. In the midst of it all sat a small brown puppy, all alone and shivering in the darkness. It cried out again and again with its tiny voice, but the sound was only lost in the howl of the wind. The puppy cried out once more, with his little tail tucked between his legs, he sought shelter from the wind.

Nearby was a house, warm and inviting. Light was streaming out of the windows into the dark night. If you listened closely, you could hear the soft crying of a child. A little girl sat looking out her window. Tears were gliding down her little round cheeks as she sat watching the street cars rush by, wishing that her beloved dog would come back to her. She closed her eyes and the horrifying scene replayed in her mind. A dog bounding into the street, the screech of brakes, a heartbreaking cry...then silence. She couldn't believe that her dog, her very best friend, was gone forever.

It was time for bed. The lights went out, the wind quieted and raindrops began to dance in the light of the streetlamps. All you could hear was the pitter-patter of the rain, the crying of a little girl, the whimper of a puppy.

The next morning, the sun rose above the city. The puppy began to limp slowly down the sidewalk. He was a puppy, alone and forgotten. He, his brothers and sisters had been sold on a street corner to people passing by and after a few hours of waiting, the last of his siblings were taken home by loving families. He felt lonely and missed his playmates but was looking forward to a new home; sadly no one came for him. He was lifted out of the box and shoved into a paper sack, then thrown into the backseat of a truck and driven into the city.

They drove through a maze of twists and turns, down alleys and across busy intersections. Finally the car stopped on a small quiet street. The sack was tossed into an alley the puppy tumbled out. He tried to run after the car but it was too fast for him. He trudged back to the small alley and there he spent the most miserable night of his life.

Meanwhile, the little girl was sitting on her porch swing, tugging at her soft blonde curls and remembering all of the memories she and her dog, Buddy, had shared. She had just moved into a little house on Rosemary Lane and didn't know anyone at all. Now, her only friend was gone and she thought that she was the only one in the whole world without a friend, but she wasn't.

Slowly, the puppy made his way down a small street. He trudged past the many houses that sat on Rosemary Lane and suddenly, he stopped. Two teary blue eyes met his own deep brown eyes and somehow, the beings behind those eyes realized that they were meant for each other.

Slowly, the tiny brown dog limped up to the girl's outstretched hand. He sniffed it then sneezed sending him tumbling into a mud puddle.

The girl covered her mouth as she giggled then went over to help. She lifted him into her arms and he licked her freckled nose with his soft pink tongue.

Suddenly, she sat him down, trying to think of a name for him. Her parents had gotten Buddy a year before she was born so she hadn't taken part in naming him and wanted to name this one herself.

All of this thinking had made her hungry so she reached into her pocket for the Hershey bar she had gotten from her mother. She reached down to ruffle the fluffy hair atop the puppy's head and grinned. As she popped the chocolate into her mouth, she realized that it was the same color as the puppy's fur and at that moment she knew what to call him...Hershey!

She reached down to hug the puppy and went twirling through the yard with him in her arms. Suddenly her mother burst through the door. She took her apron in one hand and with the other; she fiercely snatched the puppy from her daughter. The girl knew that her mother was angry so she backed away, staring at the ground.

"Christine Johnson! Haven't I told you not to play with strange dogs? I am shocked at you for disobeying me!"

She did remember her mother telling her this but hadn't thought of Hershey as a strange dog. She was not going to let Hershey go!

'*Why doesn't mother let me have Hershey?*' She thought, '*Doesn't she know how much he means to me?*'

Christine's cheeks burned fiery red as she grabbed the squirming puppy from her mother's arms.

"You will *NEVER* take Hershey!" she cried.

Her mother stepped back in utter shock. The girl darted away from her mother who marched furiously into the house, slamming the door behind her.

Once mother was gone Christine made her way out from behind the woodpile where she had been hiding with the puppy and tiptoed along the sodden grass to the window. Slowly, she opened the window so she could hear her parents' discussion.

"Frank, I really don't want another dog in the house. Buddy was enough work, but a puppy? We'll have to deal with this one chewing on furniture; wetting the carpet...I'm just not up for that! He's still a puppy and somebody is bound to fall in love with him. I'm calling the pound!"

Anger burned in the eyes of the girl as her mother picked up the phone.

'I'll never let anyone take Hershey! I'll hide in the park!'

Just as she had started down the sidewalk, rain pelted downward and fierce wind knocked her little body to and fro. Suddenly, she was smacked to the ground by a falling branch and there was a sickening crack as she hit the cement.

The puppy wriggled free from Christine's arms and scampered back to her house. He scratched at the door, barking wildly until Christine's father came.

Hershey ran toward the unconscious girl and father followed close behind. When he reached his daughter, his face paled. He took his daughter in his arms and carried her home. Suddenly, the scream of an ambulance pierced the dark night, coming closer...closer...closer...

The little girl awoke in an unfamiliar room amongst a sea of balloons. A sigh of relief was heard among the people surrounding her. She then realized that she was in the hospital with not only her family, but some other familiar faces too. Jenny, Katie, and Amy...had they all come to see *her*? Did they want to be friends? They did!

Mother bent down and whispered in her

daughter's ear, "I'm so sorry about what happened today. Hershey saved your life and…I would be honored to have him as part of our family.

Susan Nelson
7th Grade

Two Weeks of Why

The lord will provide, dear, but you must give him some help.
Sir Hugh Casson

As I walked home one day, I mulled over the school hours in my head. Test, check. Homework, check. Funny comment, check. I do this every day -- find the noteworthy clips and run the highlight reel for my mother. When I climbed the basement stairs, I heard her on the phone, so I grabbed an apple and started munching. Thinking about all the homework I had to do, I half-heartedly listened to her conversation.

"Yes. Uh-huh. Two weeks? Right. Yes, well, my husband's work would have to agree, you must understand that. Okay. Can I get back to you? Thank you for your time. Goodbye." Click. The phone was placed back in its cradle.

"How was your day?"

"mfokaymeffgusesaf," I mumbled around the apple. I swallowed and tried again.

"Okay, I guess. I got a lot of homework and stuff though. This weekend, can you help me with my English paper? It's due next Friday."

"Sure."

"Who was on the phone?"

"The Red Cross."

"The Red Cross? Like, the volunteer people?"

"Yeah."

"Why?"

"Well, I'll have to discuss this with your dad but...I'm thinking about volunteering to help with Hurricane Katrina relief in Louisiana or Mississippi."

Whoa. This was a lot to swallow. I'd known about Katrina and New Orleans, of course, and had heard that there was a lack of volunteers. But I'd always assumed people who volunteered for that stuff were not married women with three kids. Maybe a New York radical who wore bandannas all the time, but certainly not my mother.

"Thinking? Not....certain yet?" I asked, trying to keep the thought of my mom wading through waist high floods from invading my brain.

She knew me better than I liked to admit.

"Not certain *yet*. But I probably will be going if I can take the required classes soon."

This wasn't so bad, I thought. She'd be making a difference. Something else struck me.

"How long would you be gone?"

My mom hesitated. She knew my reaction to this before the prison sentence was uttered.

"Two weeks."

The initial reaction — whoa — turned to "WHAT!? TWO WEEKS! ARE YOU KIDDING ME?"

"Erin, listen to me..."

I ran out of the kitchen and into the living room, where I threw myself onto the couch and buried my face in a pillow. I saw her in New Orleans, getting shot by a looter or drowning in a street full of filthy water. What if they ran out of food? What if she *never came back*?

"Erin, I won't go anywhere or do anything unsafe. I promise!"

Even if she did come back, she'd miss my soccer games and Back-to-School Night, where it was our age-old tradition for her to scout out the teachers so we could discuss them later. It just wouldn't be the same with my patient, gentle father. She couldn't go. She couldn't. I wasn't going to let her. I knew I was acting childish, but I didn't care.

She came into the living room and sat beside me. I turned my face away.

"Erin, there are people who need me much more than you do right now."

"I need you." Stubborn, as usual.

"Not as much as the people in the South need help."

Saved by the bell. I had to go to soccer practice, so our discussion was cut short. After spending a productive hour-and-a-half kicking the sense out of anything that came near me, I felt a whole lot better. I was coming to terms with her leaving. I was realizing that this was something she needed to do. It wasn't personal.

As the week wore on, I saw more signs of her departure — the Red Cross classes, the new work boots, the air mattress hauled out of hibernation, the phone calls to friends and close family, and the new Red Cross Official Volunteer T-shirts.

After saying goodbye to my mom at the airport, my dad, sisters and I returned home. I remember thinking, "Well, only two more weeks to go!"

The next night she called from a car bound for Gulfport, Mississippi, a city about 150 miles away from New Orleans. She hadn't seen any destruction yet, but she'd heard Gulfport had been hit hard. She called almost every night.

I missed her a lot, but was getting used to having my dad and grandma around more. I would be fine during the day, no matter what happened. But at night, as soon as she was on the phone, I felt tears behind my eyes.

We counted the days until her return. Whenever a setback occurred, someone would say, "It's okay. She'll be back in __ days!" It made me realize that my family has almost mythical faith in my mother.

That next Saturday, she called. My soccer team had won, 4-1.

"I scored a goal and had an assist!" I told her -- gleeful but bitter at the same time. "You weren't there to see it."

"I wish I had been. I really do. But today, we were giving out kits to help people clean up their yards, right? So I offered this guy a rake, and he said, 'I don't need it.' I looked puzzled, so he explained, 'All I've got left of my house is my front steps.'"

I blushed. Thankfully, my dad had taken over the phone and I was left to think about this -- to wonder why. Why did some people lose everything while other people got to go on with their normal routines? Why did my mom decide to go to Mississippi? Why did I miss her so much?

There were many of these little moments over the next week.

"I got an A+ on all of my progress reports."

"I met a woman who had lost her husband and daughter right before Katrina struck. Then she lost her house as well."

"Matt invited me to his birthday/Halloween party."

"I tried to get a nurse to a diabetic man who lived in a trailer. He almost didn't get a relief check."

The night before my paper was due, my mom helped me edit it while she was waiting in line for a shower. And then the two weeks that had seemed like months were over, and she was coming home.

We drove to the airport, all four of us — my dad, Carrie, Lani and me — full to bursting with excitement. We found the right baggage claim and shifted uneasily.

After, it seemed, two more weeks, my dad declared, "I see her!"

"Where, where?" All three of us burst out.

"There!"

And she was there. She was looking rather weather beaten, but she was there, and that's what counted. I hugged her, right in the terminal, even though no self-respecting 14-year-old should ever lower herself to Public Displays of Affection.

Kelly O'Foran
8th Grade

Kavita and the Diar Wolves

If you don't know the trees you may be lost in the forest, but if you don't know the stories you may be lost in life.

Siberian Elder

The children came running from all directions to greet her: to bring her gifts, to hear her tales. She sat them down in a circle and said to them, "Have you children been good little girls and boys?"

"Yes!" They all cried, "Yes yes."

"Well then," she said, "What tale do you want to hear?"

They all started yelling.

"The Bear!"

"No, the Warrior Chief!" "

"No, she told that one last time!"

And then, above the noise someone said, "The Diar Wolves," and then they were quiet. "Okay," she said, "I will tell you the story of the Diar Wolves."

And then she began:

"Like magic, pictures began to form in the heads of the children; flashes of words and color. It was a day of harvest time. The men were harvesting corn, the women storing it in baskets while the children were collecting as many nuts and berries as they could find.

Kavita, one of the smallest children decided to wander farther than usual to find the biggest nuts in the heart of the forest. She had not gone far when she spotted a cave: a huge, dark cave. And, then she saw a pair of bright yellow eyes and a huge hairy grey body of a Diar Wolf.

Kavita had been warned of these creatures. They killed deer and buffalo in five minutes; they destroyed villages and camps; and according to legend, no living creature had survived an attack of the Diar Wolves.

So, Kavita knew she had to leave before it spotted her. After she was out of earshot of the cave, she ran into the village to find her cousin, Two Hawks.

'Two Hawks! Two Hawks!' she cried.

Two Hawks, a tall thin man with grey eyes turned as Kevita came running.

'What is it, Kavita? What do you want?'

'Two Hawks,' she gasped, 'I saw them – the Diar Wolves.'

'Kavita,' he started.

'Kavita!' her mother cried, 'What are you doing here? Where are your nuts?'

'Mother,' she said, 'I have seen them. I have seen the Diar Wolves.'

'Nonsense,' her mother said, 'There are no more Diar Wolves this side of the mountain. Don't be foolish.'

'But I've seen them,' she persisted.

'I don't want to hear any more of this Kavita. Now get back to work.'

But Kavita did not get back to work. Instead she turned and headed toward the largest long house: the home of Kalutsa. Kalutsa was the Wise Man of the village. Everyone went to him for advice or so he could tell the meaning of their dreams. He was thought of among most as a man of great knowledge and understanding. Kavita thought he would help.

She walked into the long house and there sitting besides a fire smoking a pipe was Kalutsa. When she told him her story he said, 'There are no more Diar Wolves. I myself helped to kill them.'

'But I've seen them,' she persisted.

'Go back to work,' he said and this time she listened.

That night they came: at least eight of them to attack. Kavita's village tried hard to defend themselves but many people died. Those who survived went to join a neighboring tribe and eventually joined the League of 5, which is our tribe today.

"And with that, she left: Kavita the storyteller. The children sat in a confused silence.

"Aren't stories supposed to end happily?" asked a small child.

"Yeah," said another, "And how come people died? That isn't happy."

"Well, I guess we won't know until she comes back. Come on! We'd better get back to work."

And with that they left.

Brenna Rivett
7th Grade

Lost In Manhattan

I think we may safely trust a good more than we do.
Henry David Thoreau

On the East Side of New York City, in a cozy apartment on 32nd street, one family was very busy.

"Wake up, Susan!" Mother shouted through the hall. "It's 8:30! Today we're going shopping in Manhattan, remember? Hurry dear, get dressed quickly and eat your breakfast. We have to catch a taxi to get to Macy's early while they still have a good selection of dresses on sale!"

Twelve-year-old Sarah had been patiently waiting all week to go shopping with her mother. She was going to be a flower girl in her cousin Rebecca's wedding and her mom was going to buy her a fancy dress.

After dressing, Susan brushed her long blond hair into a ponytail and made her bed. After eating her breakfast of cinnamon-sugar toast and orange juice, she and her mother hurried out to the sidewalk, lined with bare maple trees, to catch a taxi. Her mother hailed a taxi and Susan took a seat by a window. As she looked out the window, Susan caught glimpses of people jogging, walking their dogs, ordering food at hot dog stands and hailing taxis. Susan watched all the buildings disappear behind them as they drove towards Fifth Avenue.

After fifteen minutes, the taxi stopped in front of Macy's. Susan's mother paid the driver and they walked into the red-carpeted entrance of the department store. After an hour of looking, Susan still had not found the perfect flower girl dress. Her mother decided that they might find a pretty dress at another department store on Fifth Avenue. Disappointed, Susan solemnly followed behind her mother outside to the hustle and bustle of Manhattan.

Susan suddenly stopped in front of Tiffany's, a glittering jewelry store. 'Just look at the size of that diamond ring! It's almost as big as my thumbnail. I bet it costs a million dollars!' she said to herself.

In between a T-shirt vendor and a hot dog stand, Susan spotted an ice cream shop. 'Oh, if I only had a triple scoop of mint chocolate chip ice cream cone with fudge syrup and sprinkles!' Susan thought to herself.

"Oh, please Mother, can you buy me a cone?"

There was no answer. Susan turned to look, but her mother was nowhere to be found.

Susan cried in despair, "Mother, Mother where are you?"

As Susan realized that her mother hadn't stopped to admire the jewelry with her, she frantically called her mother's name. But it was no use. The crowd of people all around was strange and unfamiliar to her.

"Mother!" she yelled, even though she knew it was no use.

"This is not good. What will I do?" she asked herself as she stopped running. I don't know how I'll ever find her."

Susan began walking down Fifth Avenue quickly searching to see if her mom was in one of the stores. She entered a cramped china shop but her mom wasn't there. Susan poked her head in a brightly lit cosmetics store, but she had no luck there either. She visited many other shops, but her mother was gone. Her feet were sore and her head was spinning.

"If I walk around this block, maybe I'll find her," Susan convinced herself.

As she was searching the block, a sidewalk stand selling colorful scarves and purses caught her eye.

"I could buy a matching violet scarf for my best friend René," she thought.

Susan was wearing the one she had recently gotten for her birthday. She searched through the mountains of different colored, fluffy scarves. After she had looked through the whole bin and still couldn't find a purple scarf, Susan walked away with sagging shoulders.

Suddenly a deep voice shouted "Hey, you!"

Susan turned sharply.

"Who, me?" Susan asked, alarmed.

"Put that scarf back in the bin if you aren't going to buy it!" the man said, revealing his local accent.

"No, no this is mine; my dad bought it for me!" Susan sputtered.

"Listen girl, that scarf is mine and you didn't buy it," the vendor snarled.

Susan told him determinedly, "Mr. I didn't steal it, it's mine."

The man started coming toward her. Susan broke out into a run and nearly knocked over a woman pushing a stroller. Susan, scared and trembling with fright, turned a corner. The angry vendor stopped to get a police officer and the two started off again to chase Susan. Quickly, she sprinted into an alley and ducked behind a dumpster.

"Whoa, that was close, too close," she breathed a sigh of relief.

Susan looked at her watch.

"Oh my gosh, it's 12:45! I have been lost for two hours! I have got to find Mom somehow."

For a few moments she stood, thinking frantically. Suddenly, she snapped her fingers,

"I've got it! Mom always said if you get lost, you should go back to the place where you got separated. When I couldn't find Mom, I was at that jewelry store, Tiffany's, with the sparkling diamonds. That's probably where I'll find her!" Susan shouted happily.

She walked around the block, searching for the jewelry store. She spotted it just around the block. And there standing by the entrance was her mother on her cell phone, a frantic expression on her face.

"Mom! Mom! I found you!" Susan cried happily as she ran and hugged her mother.

"Oh Susan, you gave me such a fright!" her mother told her. From behind Susan's mom came a gruff voice.

"Hey, you were the one who stole my scarf!"

It was the vendor who Susan had run from, and he was with the same police officer who had chased Susan!

"Mother," Susan cried in distress, "Can you tell this man that I didn't steal my scarf, please."

Susan's mother looked confused, but answered, "No, this scarf belongs to her, her dad bought it for her birthday."

The scarf man was very embarrassed.

"I'm dreadfully sorry, ma'am--I thought that the scarf was mine. They look exactly the same," he said in an apologetic tone of voice.

"That's all right," Susan told him. Susan and her mother smiled and bid him a good day.

Shortly after, when Susan and her mom had finished lunch, Susan remembered;

"Mother, I still want to buy a purple scarf for René."

They walked back to the vendor stand selling scarves and purses.

Susan said, “Hi, it’s me again. Do you have any purple scarves left?”

The vendor, grinning, pulled out a soft fluffy purple scarf from a box under his stand.

Susan gasped, “It’s perfect! Thank you.”

Susan paid for the scarf with her own money.

“Let’s go to the ice cream shop.” Her mom suggested, “I’m craving for a double scoop of strawberry ice cream.”

Susan was delighted.

“Let’s go!” she cried.

When they were enjoying their ice cream, Susan’s mom remarked, “You know Susan, it’s been a long day. Let’s go shopping for your dress next weekend.” Susan completely agreed.

Rachel Soltis
6th Grade

The Book That Told the Future

The more that you read, the more things you will know. The more that you learn the more places you will go.

Dr. Seuss

Maddie Kim never read a good book in her entire life. She read books, but never got past the first chapter. But June 18, 1999 is when it all happened. Maddie had just ended school. It was summer vacation in Virginia.

“Bye, Mad, see ya in eighth grade after summer’s over,” yelled Maddie’s best friend, Callie, from the bus as Maddie got off bus 419.

Her house was a few houses away from the bus stop, so it wasn’t a long walk home, but for some strange reason, Mrs. Kim was sitting in the running station wagon.

“Mom, what are you doing here? You’ll embarrass me in front of my friends!” Maddie scowled at her mother.

“Well, first get in and I’ll tell you,” her mother replied. The bus with roaring kids drove away and Mrs. Kim put the car in drive.

“Mom!” Maddie yelled.

“All right, I wanted you to pick out a book at the library to read this summer,” said Maddie’s mother as she put the left blinker on. The car was silent. Not a word came from either of them. Mrs. Kim put the car in park and took out the key. The engine stopped.

"Well, let's go." Maddie's mother was anxious because she wanted some books to read too.

"I'm not going!" Maddie boomed. She kept her seatbelt on with her arms crossed, "You can't make me."

But Mrs. Kim had ways. The next thing she knew, Maddie was in the library staring at her watch.

"Is it time to go now?" Maddie huffed.

"Why don't you go pick out a book? The Dr. Suess books are on that shelf over there." Maddie's mom sounded serious.

"You're joking, right?... I'm not that young, Mom!!! Fine, I'll go over here."

"Please promise you'll get a book that you won't just read the first chapter," her mom replied. It was too late. Maddie was out of site.

"Fantasy, fantasy, oh....what's this?" Maddie was browsing the shelves and something caught her eye. "*The Adventures...of You.*" Maddie read the title out loud.

"Shh," an old man sitting at a table whispered to her, but she paid no attention. The book was dusty when she took it off the shelf. It was blank on the front and back of the book. Just the title was on the spine. With the title a date was written, 1775. The color of the book had faded, but you could tell it had been a navy blue.

"No one's read this book in a while." Giggling at the thought, Maddie opened to the back of the front cover. It said, "Your journey begins if you can read this."

"Whatever," Maddie shrugged.

That afternoon, she sat on the bouncy sofa with the book in her hands. The fire was crackling in the fireplace. A lamp was beside her and the blinds were down. The fire warmed the room with comfort. Maddie opened to the first chapter.

She read out loud, “Chapter One. If you survive to Chapter Two.”

“Once upon a time a boy/girl like you, lived like you, in a town like you, in a house like you. If you stop reading this book, something will happen to you!”

“What does that mean?” Maddie whispered as chills ran down her spine.

“Oh, no! I stopped reading,” Maddie whispered again giving her more chills. She closed the book throwing it on the floor.

The book with the strange title flew open, caused by a gust of wind! Maddie crouched on the sofa not knowing what was happening or would happen next. The wind seemed to come from no where. Whoosh, the fire blew out, with a little sparkle to it. The room grew cold. The lamp went out! The light bulb exploded! Tiny glass pieces flew to the floor missing Maddie by an inch! The room was swallowed into the darkness that awaited in the corners. Then it was still.

Maddie looked outside hoping to see the sun, but instead the sky was green. A grey shape slid out of the clouds.

“A tornado!” Maddie screamed!

Objects were flying in every direction. Boom! A flying stick cracked the window. More glass missed the screaming Maddie!

“What’s happening?!”

Maddie panicked. She jumped off the couch stepping in glass and ran to the bathroom across the hall. It had no windows in it and was in the center of the house. She flipped on the switch. She saw a toilet, sink, carpet, and snakes! Her screams were flattened by their hissing and rattling! The snakes started to slide up her socks, but Maddie was out of there before one could bite her.

“A tornado, snakes! What’s causing this? Where can I hide,” she cried! The basement!

Maddie almost tripped running down the steep stairs. She closed the basement door, locking herself in. She fell on the floor crying, tears rolling down her cheeks. Her back was welcomed to warm, heavy breathing. Maddie dared not to look behind. It was a pack of snarling, growling wolves with large teeth and foaming mouths looking at her with glowing eyes.

Maddie almost pulled the door off trying to get out of there. She ran upstairs, tripping over the book. Wolves running after her, snakes slithering toward her and a tornado flying directly at her.

"The book!" Maddie grabbed the book and threw it in the ashes that once was a fire. A page caught fire and the navy blue book flew up in flames. The wolves about to grab her vanished.

The snakes starting to slither up and bite her vanished. The tornado taking up the sky heading for her house vanished. Everything disappeared!

Amy Stegeman
6th Grade

Goodbye

In each family a story is playing itself out, and each families story embodies hope and despair.

Auguste Napier

I didn't think it would make a big difference, but it really did. It was not as hard as it was with my oldest brother, Rickey. This is a lot different than I thought and I miss him so much. We never spent a lot of time together, but I just miss saying, "Hi!" to him everyday. I'll tell you what I'm talking about. My oldest brother, Rickey, is eight years apart from me. My second oldest brother, Bobby, is six years older than I am. They both went to college and I felt so sad, but when Bobby went to college, it was a bigger change than I was expecting.

First, about Rickey. Rickey and I were not very close, because he is eight years older than me. It really did not feel that we were brother and sister. It felt that we were just friends because he was so much older than I was. For example, when he was a teenager, I was just five years old. Not only that, but when Rickey went to college, he was only 45 minutes away. He came back a lot. He came back so much because of his girlfriend. He spends more time with his girlfriend, Katherine, than he does with me. I am not saying that he is not sweet, he is very sweet. He is just like another father. When my dad was out of town once, Rickey took me to a father-daughter dance.

We both could not dance which made it a bunch of fun! When he left for college, it wasn't a very big change for me because I was not use to having him around and doing a lot of activities with him. I still missed him and, when he came back, I enjoyed having him here.

My second oldest brother, Bobby, was a lot of fun and we were closer than Rickey and I, maybe because we were closer in age. When we were younger, we were pretty close but Bobby and Rickey were the close ones. They would do everything together. They were best friends almost like they were the same person.

Bobby was always nice to me. He never picked on me. I do remember this one time. The boys always had trophies for basketball and I was too little to get trophies. Bobby made up this basketball championship for me. We went out in the garage and got all the wood and made trophies for the series of games. We used it all and he put one of his basketball men on top of the championship trophy. We had about ten games and we made trophies for each game. Bobby won all the games but the let me win the last one. He was the best basketball player ever but, when we had the game, he let me win but made it seem like I had beat him. I was so happy because I finally had a trophy and had won the championship. He made me feel so special.

For the last couple of years, Bobby and I drifted apart. I never saw him much mostly because he had a lot of close friends the last couple of years of high school and he always did things with them. When Bobby left for college, it was not like when Rickey left, this was a bigger change for me because his college was farther away and I didn't see him at all and I was so much closer to him than Rickey. I missed saying, "Hi!" to him everyday. I was sad that he was gone and I just wanted to see him.

Cliff is my third brother. We are three years apart so I am closer to him than my other brothers because we do more things together. Cliff is not in college. He can be annoying and a big tease but sometimes he can be really sweet. When we are playing sports, he gives me a head start or lets me win. In the beginning of games, he lets me get five points ahead and then he tries harder to win. Sometimes I lose, sometimes I don't but he always lets me get close. If I mess something up, he will give me his things. He's a typical brother in some respects.

It is going to be very hard when Cliff leaves for college because he is really smart and has a chance of going far away and I am so use to having him around all the time. He is the person I play with, fight with, and watch TV with. I am going to be so sad when he leaves because he is the last brother I have. When they come home from college, I am really excited to see them but it is just not the same as it used to be.

Every brother makes fun of their little sister, but they love them deep down inside and they show it by doing nice things for them when other people aren't watching. It gets sadder and sadder as each of my brothers leave. I can't imagine how I will feel when Cliff leaves, but it will be awfully sad to walk down the hall and see all those empty rooms.

Christine Stroup
7th Grade

True Friends

Truth and tears clear the way to a deep and lasting friendship.
Unknown

"Did you hear that she took seventh grade *three* times before just *barely* passing?"

Another rumor spread through the halls of Greenly High. This was only one of dozens of cruel ones just like that. This particular one was now passing over the lips of a short, blonde haired freshman girl who seemed to know a lot on the subject.

"Oh my gosh, I heard about that!" her friend, who was not much taller than her, responded, "Do you think it's true?"

"Shh, she's coming this way!"

A taller, brunette haired sophomore had just walked past. She wore ripped jeans, a blue *roxy* t-shirt, and a brown corduroy jacket. She pretended not to notice the two awe-struck freshmen, but they were hard to miss, just standing there while the rest of the student body seemed to be moving. Of course, these weren't the only people talking about her. No, she knew that they all were, behind her back – only the dumb ones did it in front of her.

"Michelle!"

The girl turned around. Another sophomore girl, a little taller than the first, came running down the hall.

"Hey Beth, the girl, who seemed to be named Michelle, said very nonchalantly. She then started walking again.

Bethany, who was now trying to catch up to her, sighed from exhaustion.

"So," she said as she finally caught up, "how are you today?"

Michelle didn't stop walking – though she heard more whispers – all she did was smile one of her many sarcastic smiles and said, "Oh my life is just great! And you know what made it so great? This morning the whole varsity football team "booed" me as I came in to school because they think that I'm a witch and put a spell on their stupid quarterback to make him break his leg!"

Bethany rolled her eyes.

"Just ignore them. Most of those rumors aren't true anyway; they'll figure it out eventually."

"None of them are true!" Michelle snapped back. She could feel tears forming in her eyes.

Bethany, who could sense what was coming, quickly responded, "We both know that, but they don't. So just ignore them, they're jerks."

Well, that didn't make it any better as much as it made it worse. Suddenly water poured out of Michelle's now blood-shot eyes – like big wet raindrops.

"I'm sick of all this!" she cried, "Why does this have to happen to me?"

Bethany bit her lip in pity.

"It's okay, Michelle. Forget about them," she said as she hugged her friend, letting her cry on the shoulder of her brand-new sweater.

As they stood there – right in the middle of the hallway – Bethany heard whispers of cruel words.

"What a loser."

"I can't believe she's crying in school, what a dork."

"She's so stupid. Why is she crying in the hallway?"

Bethany looked around cautiously. She saw the eyes of her classmates – the same classmates that yesterday were commenting on her wardrobe, but now were looking at her like she was an alien that had come from a distant planet. She couldn't help thinking if they were talking about her too. She didn't want them to. She hated it when people talked about her. She didn't like not knowing what they were saying, whether it was good or not.

She stayed there though – right in the middle of the hallway – until the bell, until she knew Michelle was okay. She wasn't going to let her best friend suffer alone. She wasn't going to let peer pressure ruin her life, like so many others had. Michelle was her friend and she couldn't just leave her when she needed her. That's why she did what she did when their friendship was tested.

After school the hallways seemed deserted. Bethany stood alone among many cold, metal lockers. She had stayed after for band rehearsal, so she was now collecting her books and such. She had just closed her locker when she heard two girls coming down the hallway – Amy and Ashley – she knew them both from band. She had planned to quietly pass them and be on her way, but their plans seemed different.

"Eww, look at that ugly sweater she's wearing," Bethany heard Amy whisper – she seemed unaware to the fact that Bethany was standing within earshot. Though when she did she just smiled sweetly, "Oh hi, Bethany!" she said happily, acting like she was excited to see her, like she wasn't just seconds ago, trashing her.

"Hey," Bethany quietly responded. Her worst nightmare had come true, they were talking about her too – they must have known she was the only one there.

"It was such a shame to see Michelle crying today," Ashley said, pretending to care, though Bethany knew that she was just making fun of Michelle.

"Yeah," Bethany said, then with a boost of courage she added, "But if you care so much, why didn't you see if she was okay?"

This seemed to have stumped the two girls. They stood there, now glaring at Bethany. Finally Amy spoke.

"You know what? I can't believe you're even friends with her. If I were you I would ditch her to save yourself from embarrassment. She's such a loser. I hope you know that."

That's when it happened. For a split-second – the longest split-second of her life – Bethany actually considered that idea – that horrible idea. She didn't know why, she couldn't help it.

She couldn't help thinking of what would happen if she didn't hang out with Michelle anymore. People wouldn't talk about her; no evil untrue rumors would spread about her because of Michelle. But then what about Michelle? It wasn't her fault people were so mean. It wasn't her fault that she dumped a guy, so he spread rumors about her. So why was she caring so much about herself when Michelle was being torn apart inside because people who didn't even know her – and what was worse, by some people who did? She couldn't let that happen to her best friend.

Amy seemed to be now smirking at her own remark. Bethany looked her in the eye.

"Do you know what I think?" she said very calmly, but building up power. I think that she's not a loser, that she's my best friend. I think that you should stop talking about her behind her back, because she didn't do *anything* to you, did she? No, she didn't. Look, I don't care anymore whether or not you talk about me, but just stop talking about Michelle."

The two girls looked surprised, but then quickly changed they're expressions to annoyed. Ashley put her hand on her hip.

"And why not?"

"Because, Brittany went on, "now you have reason to talk about me, but you never had reason to talk about Michelle."

Then she walked on, farther down the hallway, then out the front doors. She didn't know what was going to happen tomorrow, or the day after that. But she did know one thing: she wasn't going to put herself before her best friend. She wasn't going to walk away when her friend needed her – she was a true friend.

Maggie Twigg
8th Grade

High School

I write entirely to find out what I'm thinking, what I'm looking at, what I see and what it means. What I want and what I fear.
Joan Didion

The Way to Town

Confusion is a word we have invented for an order which is not yet understood.

Henry Miller

"'Ello there, what's that noise?"

"I didn't 'ear anythin'."

"I'm tellin' you I 'eard somethin'"

"Maybe it 'twas a bird."

"Didn't sound like no bird ta me!"

The bickering voices drifted up the hill, and a flock of birds flew up noisily at the commotion. A head popped over the hilltop: a face that hosted an old, bedraggled beard and beady little eyes.

He held a cane and swung it back and forth before him, for he was blind. Up popped another ragged head behind him, and both were dressed in cloaks and tunics with funny little hats perched atop their heads.

"I betcha 'eard that Bingo," The first man said, and swung his cane again.

"What? The flock 'o birds? Course I 'eard that, I ain't stupid."

The second man, identified as Bingo, stomped angrily behind with his cane. He was holding on tightly to the first man's cloak, for he was blind as well.

"Coulda fooled me," The first man said, and earned an annoyed grunt from his companion.

"Where's this town agin?"

"Er, ah," Bingo stuttered. In truth, he was feeling a bit disoriented and, well, lost. But he didn't want to seem stupid, so he fudged and said, "Just up ahead, 'arry."

Harry grunted. Just then he stopped, and blind old Bingo crashed right into blind old Harry and they both ended up in a pile on the grass.

"You stupid! What'd you do that for?" Bingo cried, feeling over the ground for his cane.

They both found it at the same time and grabbed opposite ends, and were engaged in a tug of war that lasted about two minutes until Bingo stumbled over the other cane. Bingo, thinking it was a snake he had stepped on, shrieked, and let go of his end of the stick, causing Harry to tumble backwards down the hill.

Down, down, down he rolled, past a clump of bushes, between two trees, and over a little dirt road until he hit a ditch.

"I found me cane!" Bingo called from the hill top. Harry, however, was past caring.

"Are you alright, mate?" A voice said near Harry's ear.

"Am I alright? I nearly cracked me 'ead open!" Harry struggled to his feet and felt around for the other man's hand. What he found, however, was a cane.

"Oo are you? A shepherd?"

The other man laughed, and Harry heard three other voices join in.

"A shepherd??"

"We must be the sheep then!"

"Ha ha!"

The voices muddled together into one long guffaw and Harry felt quite awkward and embarrassed.

"So sorry, sir, didn't mean ta insult you."

A voice said, "'e called you sir!" And the laughter started again. By this time Harry had turned red as a beet and seriously began to think Bingo wasn't so bad after all.

"Ahoy 'arry! Yo 'o, where'd you go?"

Bingo's stick pattered the ground as he jogged down the road. Yes, he had found the road, and also the bushes, and the trees after he had ran into one of them in his haste. Harry was about to call out to him when Bingo's stick hit him in the knee, followed by Bingo himself. Down they went!

"Did you 'ear that crash, Francis?" One of the four voices said.

Harry felt a barrage of sticks prod him in the back.

"I think I found 'em!" A voice cried out. "Or else a dead deer. It's ratha squishy."

"It's me, it's me," Harry said, and climbed out of the ditch they had fallen into. "Poor ol' blind man that I am." He mumbled.

One of the voices let out a gasp and said, "Aha! That makes six of us! Two more for our blind beggar club."

"I'll make some more patches!"

Bingo tapped Harry on the shoulder.

"I'm confused." He said.

Harry grunted, perplexed as well.

"Uh, sorry but we don't 'ave time to join a club. You don't by chance know where 'Ippodown might be?"

The voices seemed to huddle together. Bingo tapped his cane on the road.

One of the voices, supposedly Francis, finally said, "'Ippodown? We've been tryin' to find that town for three days now. A bit tricky, eh?"

He sounded embarrassed.

"Idon't feel so bad now." Bingo said happily.

Harry was depressed.

"Oh well, never mind then."

Francis perked up.

"Then you'll join our club? George 'ere makes great soup!" Two of the voices agreed heartily.

"Cookin's my gift." George said.

"'ow can you make soup if you can't see?" Bingo asked. George seemed befuddled, and didn't know the answer.

Harry had had enough of these strange beggars, and said suddenly, "Off we go Bingo. I think it's that way ta town." He pointed behind him, grabbed a cane, and attempted to head in that direction.

Bingo just managed to grab Harry's cloak before he had fully disappeared into the forest. Bingo felt someone grab his cloak as well.

"Come on Francis! 'E knows the way!"

"A bit o' luck! 'old on lads!" Francis grabbed Georges' cloak, and the other two joined suit. Soon, all six were headed merrily down the road into the forest. Bingo leaned forward.

"I thought we was lost." He whispered loudly.

Harry tapped his cane in front of him and ignored Bingo. Well, if they were lost for a few days more, at least they'd have good soup.

And then he fell into a ditch.

Alyssa Davis
12th Grade

The Bracelet

The manner of giving shows the character of the giver, more than the gift itself.

John Caspar Lavatar

Jaime Thompson. If I had a nickel every time I heard that name, I'd probably have $10 by lunchtime. I'd probably make enough by the end of high school to pay for half of my college tuition, if I got a nickel every time that name was mentioned, talked about, or written down.

Not that I don't like the girl, nah, *everyone* likes Jaime. Well, at least everyone knows Jaime. No, me and Jaime used to be real close, BFFs if you will. Heck, if genes didn't have any importance, you could've called us sisters. We were inseparable, got together nearly every weekend, nothing could be better. And like an idiot, I thought that nothing could change.

Then- BAM! Just like that, we entered middle school, and old elementary alliances fell to the wayside. It's not like we hated each other; our friendship just... fell apart. We never had any classes together, and three years changes a person.

So now here I am; a nobody, a freshman, too shy to make any new friends, not that anyone would want to be my friend. She's here too, same grade, but that seems to be about all we have in common.

She's surrounded by a group of friends and in her own band. She plays second guitar, I think; I wouldn't really know; I haven't talked to her in so long. Anyway, in her own band, lots of friends, boyfriend, Miss Popular, you know the type.

But you know what the worst part is? Me; sitting someplace against the wall, looking at all her friends, secretly wishing that it would all just melt away and I'd get my friend back. Nothing could've prepared me for when it actually did.

The whole thing started on a Tuesday, I think. It was a simple enough day in early October. I had come in early to do a little extra work I forgot about. Just minding my own business, sitting against the cold metal lockers, trying to find the quadratic formula in my math book, when she came up to me.

"Hey," she said, sitting down.

"Hey," I replied.

"What's up?"

"Nothing, just doing a little math homework."

"Cool."

We sat in silence against those lockers 'til the bell rang.

Jaime grabbed her book bag, said "See ya!" and left for her first class.

I also had to go to class, wondering what in the world just happened. I guess you could describe it as when you get a good grade on a test you didn't study for.

So, scenes like that ended up lasting a few days, with us just sitting there against the lockers. Over the weekend, she actually called my house, just to chat. I don't think I'll ever know how she remembered my phone number after all those years. We talked for a little while, then she hung up and we each went about our weekends.

Monday was different. Monday Jaime actually found my table in the cafeteria. We talked, ate, and laughed, just like the old days. Then it occurred to me, she seemed so...distant. And why had she just started talking to me, out of the blue? I finally got the courage to ask what was up.

"Oh Tracy, it's awful! The band is breaking up, and there's so much tension. I can't take it! Right now you're my only friend."

Her voice softened, and I could tell she was on the verge of tears. But that couldn't abate my anger. I hate to admit it, but I was furious!

"Yeah? And what about me? Do you expect me just to take you in? You left our friendship without a second thought!"

At that moment, I leapt up from the table and ran out of the cafeteria. Once I was in the bathroom, I burst into tears. How could I have been so stupid? Why criticize her for not being a good friend when she's the one who needed help? Man, I am such a hypocrite! I had one shot with being a friend, a good friend, to Jaime again, and I blew it!

It was quite awhile before I could face Jaime again. I felt so guilty; she was sitting alone at lunch now, looking absolutely miserable. It wasn't until Friday that I figured out how to apologize.

I called her house and told her that I was sorry. I asked her that if she would give me a second chance, to meet me in the park Saturday, around noon.

Sure enough, I was only waiting about three minutes Saturday afternoon when she came trudging down the path.

"Hey," she said, though not in her normal, cheerful manner.

“Hey,” I replied, matching her tone, “You hungry?” I pulled out a basket.

“Sure,” she said, “What is this, a picnic?”

“Yep,” I handed her a sandwich, “Peanut butter, banana, and marshmallows; your favorite.”

“Thanks,” she took the sandwich.

So, in short we forgave each other for our various deeds of bad friendship. We stayed at the park for hours, talking about the almost four years that we missed of each other’s lives. As we got up to leave, Jaime pulled a purple and blue bracelet out of her pocket.

“You left this at my house, all those years ago,” she said, handing the bracelet to me.

On her wrist, I could see a green and pink one.

“My friendship bracelet,” I said, tying it around my wrist. We laughed again and slowly walked out of the park, just as the sun was setting.

Rachael Roman
9th Grade

Anywhere but Home

The guardian angels of life sometimes fly so high as to be beyond our sight, but they are always looking down on us.
Jean Paul Richter

My breathing was ragged, and my lungs felt like they were on fire, but there was no way that I was ever going to stop. My battered, hole-covered old sneakers slapped against the wet pavement, sloshing water everywhere. The rhythm of my pounding footsteps was beating out a single thought. *Never going back. Never going back. Never going back.*

My legs were wobbling. My back hurt, my head was pounding, and my toes were numb with the cold. But I wouldn't stop. Couldn't. No way I would ever--

Suddenly, my treacherous legs gave out underneath me, and I went sprawling in a puddle of freezing, oily water. I gave a cry as the asphalt painfully scraped against my knees and elbows. For several minutes that's where I lay, huddled on my side and gasping for air like a beached fish. Finally, I rolled over onto my back and stared up at the murky night sky.

I couldn't hear my pursuers anymore. Heck, they'd probably stopped chasing me miles ago. It looked like I had been too darn stupid to notice. Not that I had been frightened. I'm not afraid of anything. I just know when to fight and when to flee.

My name is Lief. Lief Brigand is what I call myself. I'm average, almost boring in appearance, and if I had grown up in a normal house, with a normal family, I would have been considered a normal child. But I'm no normal child. I'm the Wolf Girl.

You see, being the Wolf Girl means I'm not normal-looking at all. I have gray, black, and white tattoos on my face, arms, and calves that look like fur. I wear contacts that have yellow irises and slits for pupils. And, weirdest of all, I have long, luxurious whiskers sprouting out of my upper lip. They're Teflon implants, but from the way people stare at me, you'd think they were real. How in the world did a girl like me end up like this? It started back when I went to live with my uncle, Lucas Farve, when I was a little over eighteen months.

Lucas ran a traveling sideshow act on the Jersey shore. It was a throwback to the traditional attraction you could find back in the older days. He would swallow swords and whatnot, and his wife, Fliea, breathed fire. John Michal was our strongman, Hera walked on tightropes, Ulric was a daredevil, and I and Katrina the Tiger Lady finished off our little group.

Lucas had five wolves, mostly tamed, and he told me I used to play with then all the time when I was little. I learned how to train them and teach them tricks like dogs. Audiences always were held spellbound by me, as Lucas would announce that I “lived with and was raised by wolves”. I didn't care that I was a real moneymaker, or that I knew nothing of the outside world. Those wolves were the only friends I had, and the only friends I needed.

Then, like all animals eventually do, the wolves died, leaving me in a precarious position. Until Lucas was able to get his hands on another couple of pups, he was without a major attraction. He began to spend more and more of his money on drink, and would often curse and scream at me for not pulling my weight. The final straw came when one night, after a lousy performance, he threw a brick at me and gave me a concussion. The next night, I packed the few things I owned, put on the most normal clothes I could find, and ran away, telling only Katrina, my sole friend in the group.

So there I was, hungry, tired, and without a clue of where I was, lying in a puddle in some godforsaken alley in the middle of the night. Maybe running away hadn't been the greatest idea after all... *What, you want to go back already? What are you, a quitter? Lief Brigand never gives up.* I heaved myself up on shaking legs, making my head spin, and made my way to the street.

It was dark and silent in the streets of this city. The only light came from glowing puddles of yellow cast by streetlights, or from the headlights of the occasional passing car. The only sounds were of the chill autumn wind gusting by, the rustle of old papers or dry leaves, and the mews of stray cats. Shivering, I pulled my tan duster closer around my body, and shoved the old fedora I had stolen from Lucas down farther on my head. This getup made me look a little like a spy from some kind of the old-timey movie, but at least it helped cover some of my stranger features. I slung my pack over my shoulder determinedly and took my first steps to freedom. *Never look back...*

My footsteps seemed to echo in dark, silent night as I started off down the lonely sidewalk. I paused to turn my collar up against the cold, and a thought struck me. There was no way I would get anywhere on foot. And with only seventy-two dollars in cash in my pocket, it didn't look like I would last long at all. An idea occurred to me just then, one so absurd and against my standards that there was nothing else to do but try it. *What the heck. What will happen, will happen.* With a sigh, I walked over to the curb, set my bag down, and waited for a car. When one drove by moments later, I leaned over and stuck out my thumb. The driver, a man in what looked like his late seventies, stuck out his own choice finger and sped by, leaving me right back where I was. *Looks like it's gonna be a long night...*

After a quick succession of cars, I was starting to get discouraged. The people that didn't completely ignore me would either try to run me over or spray me with muddy street water. *One last car. The next one is the last try.* I told myself. *Okay, maybe two more cars. But after that, I'll give up. I'll keep walking.*

Soon enough, I heard the sounds of an engine and stuck out my thumb once again. To my absolute surprise, a miracle occurred. The car, a nice-looking Lexus I wouldn't have been allowed to even touch years ago, pulled over, and the driver rolled down the window on the passenger side.

"Little late for hitchhiking, isn't it?" A pleasant, middle-aged woman sat at the wheel. I tried to look as innocent as a newborn lamb without showing her my face.

"Oh please, ma'am," I smoothed down my rough voice, meant more for shouting at animals than for talking with people, as best I could. "Please, could I just hitch a ride with you? It's just so very cold out, and don't... eh... I need to... I need a ride."

The woman smiled at me in a motherly way. "Get in, honey. Where're you headed?"

It's a new day... Never look back... I smiled to myself.

"Anywhere."

Jen Coate
9th Grade

Albino

A great many people think they are thinking when they are merely rearranging their prejudices.

William James

There are two main reasons microscopic entities are unseen by the human eye. One is that they are simply too small for the naked eye to physically perceive. The other is that the frequency of light is unable to reflect from these particles due to the size of the waves against them.

Due to the large size of one brilliant man, it would be impossible for him to become invisible because of the first reason. You may ask "Why would this man wish to become invisible?" I will tell you a story that will explain his reasoning while shaming you for being a human.

Once a child was born so pale that it horrified his parents to such a degree that they abandoned him nameless on the steps of a small church. Outside of this church, he would live a life filled with constant ridicule for his awkward appearance. This boy would grow to become the "brilliant man" I have previously described to you. No, for that to be fully true, I would have to describe him to be a giant. This man was approximately ten feet tall, because of a disorder of the pituitary gland known as gigantism.

Along with this, he also had the reddest eyes and the palest skin among anyone the people of the village had ever seen. He was known to the villagers simply by his condition, “Albino.” Tired of the ridicule and disgusted glares, he created an extremely simple form of invisibility. Using a low-frequency light which he then would shine upon himself, he was able to achieve absolute visual insignificance, at the cost of having to carry a 300 pound load of equipment everywhere, he would travel with it. He would never again be seen by those that were so disgusted by him.

One day Albino, wishing for a peaceful walk through the village in which he could be spared the pain of the stares of the villagers, heard a cry from one of the local farming fields. Struggling to carry the weight of the invisibility device over a steep incline, he passed into the field to see what was afoot. To his horror, he saw an old man crying over a dead ox. Placing the instrument upon the soil, he went to the man. The man screamed and slowly calmed down to accept his death. Albino did not kill the man. The giant, realizing that the old man would be unable to till the soil without his ox, took the plow himself. Selflessly destroying the invisibility device, Albino salvaged the materials required to provide clasps for the plow. With his extraordinary strength, he prepared the entire field before the man. With a warm countenance and shrieks of glee, the old man thanked Albino; he was both surprised and overjoyed to see such kindness from another.

While the old man was thanking Albino, a group of people from the village that had spotted the excitement approached and, ignoring the old man’s pleas to not harm the giant, captured “the beast” and took him into the town to be jailed for allegedly invading private property and for killing the ox.

Humans are always ready to note the evils and differences in this world, but they are often unable to note the good in others.

Jeremy Luc Barthélemy
12th Grade

Roman Pride

My strength is as the strength of ten, because my heart is pure.
Alfred Lord Tennyson

Cries of dying men rang through the forest. The clank of steel against steel as men struggled for their lives was like thunder in a storm. The yells of the Roman officers trying to get their men into a defensive formation were cut short as they were impaled by enemy archers. Chaos reigned as the Gaul ambush destroyed the rear of the long over-stretched legion. Markus could see this all happening as he rode with his fifty Cavalry men down the column toward the carnage.

Markus was commander of fifty elite legionnaires who had been in every conflict the empire had ever fought in the last twenty years. Markus was a classic Roman. Small, compactly built and strong, he could hold his own on a horse but was better suited to the Roman battle line. He had on the standard Roman plate armor and held a magnificent large red shield as did his fellow men. He had a pylon, a long Roman throwing spear, at his side and a short stabbing sword on his belt. The fifty he commanded were all local heroes. They had been assigned to guard the column as it moved though hostile Gaul territory. As they approached the battle, the roar of their steeds deafening, they saw the Gaul's retreat and melt away into the forest.

Romulus leaned over as they slowed to a trot and said, "They flee at the might of the Empire sir."

Romulus, Markus's second in command, was a tall proud man. He was taller than most Romans and was skilled on the horse, a skill rare in a culture where heavily armored men were the dominant military force. Both he and Markus had grown up in the rich farmland of Rome. Both had joined the legions as soon as they could and both had fought together in northern Italy against the Gauls, where they gained legendary status.

As Marcus and his men rode up to the surviving legionnaires, they were careful to steer their horses around their fallen comrades but also careful to use the dead Gauls as a carpet.

"Captain" called Marcus to one of the surviving men. "How many dead?"

"Thirty sir," the Captain called back.

The Captain proudly wore the plate armor of a Roman Centurion and held the same shield and weaponry Marcus had. He stood with the strong alertness of a veteran.

Marcus motioned to one of his men and spoke with an authoritative tone, "Go to the Head of the column and inform the General that we have wounded and are in need of rest. Me and my men will go in pursuit of the these pathetic Gauls and will likely require support, soon."

The rider nodded and rode off, up the column. Marcus knew it would be awhile before he returned, due to the fact that the column was part of one of Rome's Imperial Legions and thus thousands of men strong. The column could be seen going up a slight hill. A glorious stream of red shields and silver armor plating, shifting through the trees. A swell of pride ran through Marcus as he watched.

Marcus could not afford to wait for a reply from the general. He motioned to his men, told the Captain to wait, and road off into the forest after the retreating Gaul. It was not long before they saw the first Gauls, acting as rear guard, dash from their hiding places at the sound of the approaching stallions. Marcus knew there was no hope of catching them but still wanted an element of surprise. So he ordered his men to dismount. He ordered ten of his men to remain with the horses and the rest to follow. As they made their way threw the forest they heard the whispering of rough voices.

Marcus put up his hand to signal to his men to be quiet and to draw their swords. As they drew closer they saw a group of bare-chested Gauls covered in war tattoos, and looking anxious.

The Gauls seemed bothered by something and were trying to line up into a formation. Marcus knew this was the time to attack but something just wasn't quite right. He did not have time to think it through though. Any minute they could be spotted.

He raised his pylon, signaled to his men to do the same and shouted "for Rome!" and threw his pylon.

At the same time, all his men threw their pylons and a wall of sharp spear tipped pylons shot out of the forest and into the very surprised Gauls. The thump of steel against flesh resonated through the forest. Marcus charged. The charge smashed into to the Gauls shattered ranks.

Marcus came face to face with a Gaul, screaming from a pylon wound, and slit his throat, cutting the scream short. Another Gaul came screaming at him, sword raised. Marcus dispatched him with a vicious uppercut to the belly. The Gaul fell to the ground clutching his stomach. At the same time, Marcus blocked a sword thrust with his shield as his men attacked the Gaul from behind. Marcus stood and looked around the battle field. He saw Romulus decapitate a Gaul and lead a charge against the last straggle of Gaulic men standing. The Gauls were slaughtered by Marcus's glorious men in silver armor and brandishing red shields.

Several minutes later Romulus strode over to him and wiped his sword on the ground. Markus nodded to him and with a frown said, "Why are we here Romulus?"

"For the might of the Empire, Sir" Romulus replied

"But why here? We get caught up in the excitement of the battle and the Glory of the Empire but we don't actually know why we're here taking men's lives."

Romulus did not answer.

As they walked back, Marcus could feel something was still wrong. Near the clearing where the horses were kept they could not see their guards.

Suddenly, one of Marcus's men cried out "Sir!!"

Marcus looked over and saw one of the guards laying dead on the ground pin cushioned with arrows. With a sudden shock Marcus realized that he had not killed all the Gauls. It was a trap.

A shower of arrows shot out of the trees and slaughtered half of his men, including Romulus. The surviving men formed up behind Marcus in a magnificent Roman battle line, shields raised, and swords out. Marcus led the charge but was cut down by another hail of arrows.

As Marcus fell to the ground he saw a brilliant scarlet red and silver line cutting through the trees. The reinforcements had arrived, but too late. But as he saw this a swell of pride went through him. He realized why he was there; for something more, something great and powerful, something that would make him glorious.

These were Marcus's last thoughts before life slipped from his grasp.

Patrick Berish
9th Grade

God's Hand

Faith is the centerpiece of a connected life. It allows us to live by the grace of invisible strands. It is a belief in a wisdom superior to our own.

Terry Tempest Williams

The wind wailed and thrust up sand as it swept across the shores of the beach. Immense raindrops fell from the gray sky, smacking the tops of my golden curls. The pink ribbon that held my hair halfway up danced in the storm's wild winds. I scurried home quickly, almost tripping over the lace of my light blue dress. As our tiny beach house came into sight, I saw Mama standing on the screened-in porch looking for me.

"Come inside!" she shouted once she saw me. "Hurry!"

Once I was inside, dripping wet and cold, Mama tightly embraced me in Grandma's homemade quilt. My younger brother, Jack, enveloped in a blanket, was curled up in the cradle Papa made for him, facing the wood-burning stove. I pulled up a chair and sat alongside him. He was sound asleep; probably not even aware that our small town on Cape Cod was going through one of its worst storms ever.

“Rachel,” asked Mama, “would you please call the Balberd family and see how their poor, little shack is doing?”

“Yes, Mama,” I replied.

I rose from my seat and, hobbled by my tightly wrapped blanket, stumbled over to the phone. With stiff, cold fingers, I slowly dialed the Balberd’s phone number.

Ring. Ring.

“Hello?” asked a startled voice from the other line.

I quickly knew who it was. It was my close friend, Austin Balberd. He’s a tall, sort of slim boy for a twelve-year-old boy. His voice seemed hoarse and a bit hard to understand.

“Austin!” I shouted. “It’s me! Rachel!”

There was static in the phone, but I was still able to interpret what the poor boy was saying.

“Rachel!” he replied. “Are you and your family okay?”

“Yes, we’re fine,” I told him. “How’s your family? Is your house holding up okay?”

“Well, the tree next to our house is looking a bit rickety and…”

There was a huge crash and then silence fell over the phone. My heart jumped and I started to panic. “What happened?” I thought.

“Austin?” I screeched.

No reply. I shouted his name again and again. But each time the only thing I could hear was the rhythm of my own heartbeat growing louder in my ears.

I ran to Mama and told her the whole conversation I had with Austin. She looked worried.

“May God guide them tonight and pray that everyone is all right,” she said softly. I saw Mama stoop her head and murmur a quick prayer.

Fear overwhelmed me and I felt like crying. Something deep inside of me, though, told me that everything was going to be all right. I started to calm down. I had to be strong for Mama and Jack. I sat back down in my chair and looked over at Jack. His eyes, always bright and filled with delight and curiosity, were now open and looking straight at me. He smiled.

"Mama? Everything's going to be okay, right?" I asked softly.

She picked up her head which she had been resting on the table. A streak of tears glistened upon her soft, white face like the suns reflection on a calm river. I knew that she was concerned about Papa. I, for sure, was.

Papa had gone out fishing the night before the storm. He told me that he was going to come home before the dreadful weather arrived. The storm was supposed to hit the next evening when Papa got back, but unexpectedly came early in the morning. The calm ocean water quickly turned into to a fierce, dark blue nightmare. Mama had paced back and forth in front of the door, waiting for Papa to come back from his overnight fishing trip. But it was already late in the night and still there was no Papa.

"Yes," said Mama after a short pause. "Everything will be fine."

Suddenly, the door swung open and wind raced past, sending a cold splash of mist through our home. Standing in the doorway was the dark silhouette of a tall man. His scruffy beard dripped with ice-cold water. He was soaked to the bones.

"Papa!" I cried.

Mama ran to him and flung her arms around his neck. She began to weep.

"I'm so glad you're all right!" she cried.

"I found these people out in the storm," he said with a grin. He stepped inside and revealed Austin and his family.

"Oh!" choked Mama. "Please, come in."

We all followed Mama back into the kitchen. Tracks of mud traced back across the freshly cleaned floor, but Mama didn't care. She made a pot of tea. As she passed out blanket to everyone, there weren't enough blankets to go around, so I offered to share my blanket with Austin. We all sat in the kitchen, listening to Papa's fishing story and drinking our hot tea. Mama, now holding Jack in her arms, was smiling knowing that everyone was safe again.

"It's good that you and your family were here to provide us with a place to stay for the night," whispered Austin.

"No problem," I said. "You know you're always welcomed into our home."

Austin smiled. "It's weird," he began.

"What was?"

"When I was talking to you on the phone, there was a crash. And that tree aside our house was swaying vigorously in the storm's winds, and just snapped. But, it didn't crash into the room that we were in. Every other room was either buried in rubble or had a few branches coming through the ceiling. Father said it was a miracle from God," replied Austin.

"That's amazing!" I exclaimed. "God must really be looking over you."

"Yeah," said Austin, "He's probably looking after both of our families, making sure that we are all together and safe."

I smiled at him. "That's exactly it," I said softly.

He smiled back at me and put his arm around my shoulders. I knew then that whatever was to happen to us, we were all in it together in God's hand.

Sarah Efthim

9th Grade

Halloween Murder

The best murder stories are often soufflés: lightly, delicately flavored and sometimes threatening to fall.

Katrine Ames

There once was an old man who lived in a house atop a hill. Theodore Ainsworth was the name by which the whole town knew him. It was common knowledge that he had received a huge inheritance, and it was hidden in his attic, but few would have searched for it. He was just such a nice old man, who would've wanted to do such a thing? Theodore was the one children went to for hot chocolate after school in the winter; Easter eggs in April; the best candy on Halloween. However, besides knowing of his generosity and kindness, little background had been gathered concerning him. In fact, there were only two people who had any other information about him.

"So, are you willing to take the job?" Mr. Morris asked Rebecca. He was whispering to the fifteen-year-old over the counter. A cash register, some change, and a bottle of pills sat between them. The girl, decked out in green shirt and jeans, smiled.

"Sure. When?"

"Oh, sometime soon."

"Just for my sense of drama, how does late Halloween night sound?"

"Perfect."

The elderly Theodore was sitting in a rocking chair on the porch on October 31. Dusk had just set in, and with it came the flood of goblins with lopsided horns, vampires who'd gotten tired of fake teeth and princesses in sneakers. It was nearly eleven before the inundation trickled to an end. With a long sigh, the old man rose and stepped back into his dark cottage. He creakily settled into an equally creaky bed and lay in the darkness for a few moments.

Far in the distance, the occasional screech or pound of knocking on a door met his ears, but for the most part, it was fairly quiet. The usual groans and humming found in all old houses soothed him almost to sleep. His inner peace was disrupted by a sudden swish of cloth that he was not accustomed to. A stray trick-or-treater? He thought not; no doorbell rang, nor tapping on the front door. Another swish sliced another gash in the traditional sounds of night.

Theodore sat up slowly. His eyes were wide open, but it did little good in the black room. His left hand fiddled with the drapes by his bedside, sweeping them aside to let in a bit of moonlight. Nothing out of the ordinary met his eyes. The room was sparsely furnished, carpet-less, and separated from the rest of the house with a closed door. As expected, the window was latched tightly. Not even a breath of chill could creep in. When no further swishes were made, Theodore slipped back under the covers and shut his eyes again. The tricks children come up with was the main focus of his brain as it gradually drifted out of consciousness.

He didn't have the opportunity to entirely fall asleep, however. He heard a slight thump followed by a moan from a floorboard that only made noise when weight was put upon it. Another shuffle of fabric came, though this time it was much closer than before. Theodore's eyes snapped open again. They immediately noted a presence at the foot of his bed. It was clad all in black, complete with cape and hood. The grim reaper? No—the face was pale, but moonlight made the eyes peeking out glitter blue. Of course, the tell-tale sign was that there was no sickle. The only thing in the gloved fingers was a revolver. Theodore's eyes widened. He looked from the weapon to its wielder. With the slightest of smiles, Rebecca shot him.

Stacey Johnson
9th Grade

A Miserable Place

Dreams are necessary to life.

Anais Nin

You wake up in the middle of the night shivering uncontrollably. You reach down feeling for your sheets and a blanket in the darkness, but realize you are no longer in your bed. A stone floor has replaced your nice soft mattress. The air temperature is cool, but it feels much colder sitting on the damp, slimy floor. You run your fingers through your hair and down your shirt sleeves, and notice that they are also damp; almost as if you had broken into a cold sweat. The smell of mildew rushes into your nostrils, and the unpleasant smell sends more shivers down your spine. The silence is almost unbearable, but far off in the distance you can hear a slow "drip....drip....dripping" noise. The sound reminds you of a ping pong ball bouncing back and forth gnawing at your every inch of patience.

Desperate to find a way out, you stretch your arms in front of you to feel like a blind man for the door. Stumbling around in the pitch blackness you realize that the room is very small, but has a high ceiling. You spread you arms like wings and are able to skim the opposite walls with the tips of your fingers. The walls have a smooth, slippery texture, like algae covered rocks at the bottom of a pond. You search the whole room, helplessly crawling and searching every crevice for an escape. Without success you sit breathing heavily and contemplate your next move.

As you shiver in the dungeon, the dripping water begins to flow faster. The drops have now turned into a trickle. Moments later the trickling becomes a steady stream, and then finally a rushing waterfall. You are now frantic to get out of the dungeon not knowing where the water is flowing, and if the room will begin to flood. Panic begins to rush through your body like the dangerous water you hear. Then from somewhere in the room, gallons and gallons of water dump unforgivingly onto the floor. It's as if a dam has given way! There is no time to think now, you must act quickly or you will surely drown! Feeling for footholds and places to grab, you begin to climb the stone on the wall to get to higher ground. As you make it to the top, you stretch your arm for the final stone. Suddenly, you loose your footing from the rock beneath it. You grab for something but only air slips through your fingers. You land with a "SPLASH" in the frigid water below.

Jolting awake, you realize you are on the floor of your room. You must have fallen out of your bed. You then realize you really need to use the bathroom. You inhale sharply, and then breathe a sigh of relief, realizing that your miserable dream was only just a warning!

Kelsey Ann Loy
11th Grade

Fly on the Wall

A morsel of genuine history is a thing so rare as to be always valuable

Thomas Jefferson

May 1, 1776

Boy, was it hot today! I don't know how those men can take the heat on a day like this. As for me, I have my pick of hundreds of spots in the shade that are much cooler.

Today was like every other morning. I had my breakfast (day-old compost, my favorite), and was about to see if Phineaus was up when I heard the loudest debate that I had ever heard in all my life (all three months of it) coming from downstairs. I wouldn't have been surprised if all of Philadelphia had heard it! I could tell that it was John Adams and John Dickenson. I also heard Mr. Hancock trying to bring Congress to order.

Now, I had to go see what was happening. I flew as fast as I could until I got to my best lookout spot: the corner of Dr. Franklin's desk.

Since I couldn't understand what was going on, I flew to Ben's ear and asked him.

"Nothing much," he replied. "Mr. Dickenson just postponed another debate about independence proposed by Mr. Adams. When will Mr. Adams learn that nobody will listen to him?"

"Phineaus and I were thinking the same thing," I buzzed, "and he figured the only solution was to have someone else propose."

Ben's face lit up. "Now why didn't I think of that?" he whispered. "I'll tell him when Congress adjourns today." And as I flew away he added, "Phil, that's one smart friend you've got there."

"I know," and I loop-de-looped out of the room.

June 20, 1776

Since Phineaus learned Dr. Franklin liked his idea, we've gone to every meeting of Congress. Phinny's idea worked, and now Congress has been debating independence for over a month. It's been interesting to fly around and listen to private conversations without being noticed. Being a fly can really come in handy.

After debates on every side of the issue, it was decided that a document should be written stating the colonies' grievances. The document was to be written by a young man named Thomas Jefferson, a delegate from the colony of Virginia. Everyone can't wait to hear the document for the first time. We all want to tell King George what we think of him.

June 28, 1776

Today's the day! Ben said that Mr. Jefferson has finally finished writing. Phinny and I took our seats behind an inkwell on Mr. Hancock's desk and waited for the secretary to read. As he read, no one dared to move for fear they would miss something. When he came to the end everybody seemed to have turned to stone, letting the words sink in. We sat there in a daze, wondering how one man could have written something so beautiful. It was pure genius.

Finally, the secretary asked, "Does anybody have any suggestions?"

Our happiness was shattered as everybody's hand went up (Ben, Mr. Adams, and Mr. Jefferson accepted).

"Very well," sighed Mr. Hancock. "We'll listen to suggestions one at a time. Mr. Sherman will start."

"Mr. Jefferson," Mr. Sherman began. "You mention the taxes that King George has imposed upon his colonies. However ..."

At this moment, I remembered one sentence that didn't sound right. I whispered my thoughts to Phinny and he agreed with me. We decided to improve it when we heard something. Phinny and I knew instantly that it could only mean one thing: Mr. Hancock had spotted us and was about to hit us with his flyswatter!

Phinny and I took off. We darted all around. We twisted and turned, getting more and more worn out. Mr. Hancock stood there in frustration, realizing he had missed us again. He raised the flyswatter to strike again when Ben stood up and shouted, "Mr. Hancock!"

The whole room froze. No one, not even Mr. Adams, had ever heard him raise his voice before. Ben paused a moment.

"Mr. Hancock, now is not the time for swatting flies. If that is all we are to do, then King George has already won."

"I suppose you're right," Mr. Hancock grumbled, sitting down. "Darn flies."

Phinny and I buzzed our thanks as we flew upstairs. I wrote the sentence on a scrap piece of paper so we could think.

"This sentence should stand out," declared Phinny. "It should let King George know that we mean business."

"I agree. The sentence definitely needs to have more emphasis."

"What if we listed three things that we're already entitled to?"

"Well, if we're born, we're already entitled to life."

"Right, and the bell in the tower reminds us of liberty."

"Ben once told me that a man will live longer if he pursues a life of happiness."

"That's it!" I yelled. "Those are the rights we are entitled to: life, liberty, and the pursuit of happiness. If we change a word here or there..."

I frantically scribbled the changes onto the paper. When I was done I stepped back and read the new sentence to Phinny: *We hold these truths to be self-evident, that all men are created equal, that they are endowed by their Creator with certain unalienable rights that among these are life, liberty, and the pursuit of happiness.*

"Wow," Phinny said. "I couldn't have said it better myself."

"Thanks."

July 1, 1776

We asked Ben to propose our idea. He agreed to do so after everyone else had finished. Finally, Mr. Hancock said, "Now, does anyone want to make any last suggestions?"

"I do," replied Dr. Franklin. "I propose that the sentence in the sixth line be changed to this."

When he finished, a hush fell over Congress. Mr. Hancock pondered it for a moment and then said, "Well, Mr. Jefferson, do you approve of this change?"

Everyone turned to Mr. Jefferson. He stroked his chin, and after an eternity he said, “Yes. It’s what this document needs.”

“That’s settled then,” Mr. Hancock declared. “If no one has any more suggestions, then I declare this document written. Now we shall vote on it.”

The three of us silently cheered. Phinny and I couldn’t believe that our little sentence was going to become history.

The secretary called each of the colonies, asking their delegates to vote on the declaration.

With the last colony’s affirmation, the secretary said, “I now declare that this Declaration of Independence is adopted.”

Everyone in the room slowly looked at Mr. Adams.

“Well, Mr. Adams?” asked Mr. Jefferson.

“It’s done. It’s done.”

July 4, 1776

The meeting room was filled with excitement. The document sat on Mr. Hancock’s desk. Everyone was waiting for the signing to begin.

“Everyone who signs this document knows we are committing treason against King George,” Mr. Hancock began, “and I will be the first to sign.” He signed a signature so big that King George could read it without his glasses.

Each delegate then signed in turn. At this point Ben turned to us and whispered, “It’s your turn.”

“For what?” we asked.

“To sign, of course,” Ben replied. “You two made this document possible and it would be wrong if you didn’t sign it.”

So we flew up and signed our names. We thanked Ben and flew off. As we left we heard Mr. Adams ask Ben where he had gotten his ideas.

Ben broke into a smile and said, “Let’s just say I have friends in high places.”

Meredith Miller
9th Grade

Unintelligent Design

The reason why the universe is eternal is that it does not live for itself; it gives life to others as it transforms.

Lao Tzu

Mark McGainsworthy looked at the chart again. He glanced at all the others that crowded the workshop, and back at the chart.

Amazing.

It couldn't be.

Laying in front of him, on the table, was a chart of human intelligence. He'd been working on it for a while now as a hobby – New Breed Institute wouldn't have funded something like that, not with times so critical…

But he'd been curious.

Because he'd gotten interested in this sort of thing.

Using NBI's extensive databases, he'd made the same charts of other breeds as well.

Call it a hunch, but for some reason he wasn't so surprised at this outcome.

All of the intelligence charts were exactly the same.

The charts showed a curve – the least intelligent of the species on the left-hand side and the most intelligent on the right. It looked almost like the small hill that lay outside Mark's workshop –

in the middle, the average intelligences, the number of species increased. Which made sense.

But the exact same numbers?

For every species?

He sighed.

No doubt this discovery would go unnoticed.

But that was the way God had willed it, his mother would have said.

Hmm.

God.

He wondered...

What if God wasn't alone, he thought. In fact, the chances of there only being one of a species was phenomenally tiny.

And if that God had created them, in some sort of scientific experiment?

Back to the speculations of Intelligent Design. He was an agnostic, himself, but it was always interesting to think about it.

Mark turned back to the chart and began to graph the data of a llama – it was turning into the same chart as the others, relatively.

How the mind wandered, so randomly. One second he was thinking about the intelligence of all animals on Earth, the next wondering if God was real. Some subliminal link in his mind somewhere, he supposed.

Then that link popped clearly into his head.

He shivered a little as a disturbing thought hit him.

If this God was a member of a species, if he actually existed – well, what were the chances of it being an *intelligent* designer at all?

Mark pushed the thought out of his mind.

Nah.

Gerald Ossywald Dardian was known throughout his fifth-grade class as a slow student, with a strait C-average.

His worst, simplest project was for the science fair – he created a one-sun solar system, with only nine planets. Only one of those planets had inhabitants, and all the orbits were elliptical, of all things.

It was tossed in a Universe™ garbage tank, and was never seen again.

Alexandra Penland
9th Grade

The Dream

Never doubt that a small group of thoughtful committed citizens can change the world. Indeed, it is the only thing that ever has.

Margaret Mead

One day, in an area along the great Ohio River, a group of Shawnee boys were out fishing. The River had an abundance of fish that summer, so all the boys' nets were full. As the group was walking back through the woods to their village, they came across two girls carrying reed baskets with gourds in them. The boys' leader, a strong youth named Shkote The'i (Fire heart), began commenting rudely about the two girls.

He said, "Look at those two girls, why they have life so easy. All they do is work in their gardens, while we're out working hard like men!"

The other boys all joined in this torment with jabs of their own.

Now, this form of abuse had been going on for quite some time, and the elder of the two girls, known by the name of Halakwa Mi'th (Sister Star), was tiring of it.

She said to the boys, "This is no way to treat fellow people of your own tribe!" and without another word she grabbed the other girl's hand, and walked home by a different path.

That night, while laying in her family's Wegiwa (the bark covered huts the Shawnee used in summer), Hala prayed to the Grandmother Creator saying, "Grandmother, these boys have no respect for their people. They are making my life a burden; please help your granddaughters!"

As it happens, the Creator heard the girl's prayer, and she came to the boy Shkote in a dream.

She said to him, "Grandson, you are not behaving as a good example to your friends. You must change your ways; let me show you something."

Though she appeared small and frail, the Grandmother's strength was great. With arms as soft as clouds, she picked Shkote up and flew into the sky. There she showed him the huge basket that she had begun when the world was created.

"Look," said the Grandmother, "this basket represents the world. The vertical reeds you see in the basket are men of the world, and the horizontal reeds are the women. Observe what would happen if I took out the horizontal reeds."

She removed all the reeds going form east to west, and all that was left was a pile of reeds.

"You see Grandson, if there were no horizontal reeds in the basket, there would be no basket, only a pile of sticks. And the same goes for the world. If there were no women, there would be no world; as would be the case if there were no men. What I have just shown you is that all my people are equal, no matter what color, height, gender, or tribe they belong to. Humans are all creatures of the earth and every one of you deserves to have the same respect."

To this the boy replied, "I understand Grandmother, I will change my ways!"

The next day Shkote told all the other boys what had happened to him. He told them of the beautiful basket of the world in the sky, and how the Grandmother Creator had eagle feathers and blue beads in her long purple/black hair. Most importantly, he told them of the lesson he had learned. All the boys agreed that what the Grandmother Creator had said was true.

And from that day to this, the Shawnee people have been respectful to all their people - women or men.

Sarah Solano
10th Grade

Everlasting Love

The only way to pray is to pray; and the only way to pray well is to pray much.

John Chapman

“Ten o’clock, lights out,” said Miss Rachel, the head matron. Quickly, Ruth Jones slipped into bed and turned her light off. Then the tears came.

For the past year, every night was the same, wondering where her parents were, if they even cared and what would happen to her.

Two years ago, when Ruth was ten, her parents had left her with their young housekeeper to go to Europe to attend the balls and parties of their rich friends. While they were away, Miss Diane, the housekeeper, married and not wanting to keep Ruth with her, packed a few of her possessions, took her to the children’s home and left with barely a wave. She sent a letter to Mr. and Mrs. Jones telling them where she was. A year passed but still Ruth’s parents did not come for her. She did not even receive a letter. Every night Ruth cried herself to sleep. Her parents had always given her everything she needed and wanted except what she craved the most, love.

They often were away, leaving Ruth home alone with Miss Diane who, with house cleaning and such, did not have time for the lonely girl either.

Therefore, Ruth was primarily left to herself. She hardly ever saw her parents, and when they were home, they had guests over most evenings. This severely hindered a relationship between her and her parents. She often wondered if they loved her at all. She kept silent on the matter though, letting it fester in her heart until she became hurt, angry, and bitter towards them.

At the children's home, every day was the same. It seemed to Ruth like one horrible nightmare that would never end. The other children in the home seemed to take delight in tormenting Ruth on how her parents had "abandoned her." None of them had any parents, which is why they lived there. But the fact that Ruth had parents was known amongst them all and it gave them something to tease her about. As a result of this teasing, Ruth would become angry which only provoked them to more teasing. It was an endless cycle.

There was one person who somewhat brightened Ruth's dreary days. Miss Charlotte, her favorite matron, was a tall, handsome woman who always had a smile and a friendly word for Ruth. In truth, Miss Charlotte knew of Ruth's abandonment and ached for her. She prayed with all of her heart that God would give her the opportunity to tell Ruth about Him and His love for her. Ruth was too angry and hurt to hear it and Miss Charlotte never wanted to press her for fear that she would reject it. So she waited for Ruth to bring it up on her own.

One spring day, Ruth woke up with hope in her heart. Today is my twelfth birthday; maybe I will receive a letter from Mother and Father, she thought as she slipped on her red-checkered dress. At her first chance, she sneaked away after lunch to go check the mail. Skipping quickly, she reached the end of the short lane lined with brightly colored flowers. Trembling, she opened the mailbox. Sifting quickly through the mail, she looked at every envelope for her name. But alas! No letter. I must have missed it, she thought as she slowly went through them again. But to no avail, there was no letter for her. Tears sprang to her sad eyes as she shoved the bills and letters back into the mailbox. Running back up the lane, with tears streaming down her cheeks, she ran into Miss Charlotte.

With a new burst of tears she threw herself into her arms and sobbed, "I wish I had someone who loved me!"

Praying earnestly for the right words, Miss Charlotte answered gently, "Oh, but Ruth dear, there *is* someone who loves you beyond your heart's desire."

At this, Ruth raised her tear-stained face up to her and breathlessly asked, "Who is it?"

Rejoicing, Miss Charlotte answered, "His name is Jesus and He loves you so much that He was willing to lay down his life for you. He *wants* to be your Heavenly Father when your earthly father deserts you. He *wants* to be your special friend to turn to when all your hope is gone. He wants to give you what your name means, friendship."

At this, a small smile crept to Ruth's lips.

"How does he become my father and friend?" she questioned earnestly.

With joy in her heart, Miss Charlotte answered, "All you have to do is ask; He has been waiting a long time for you to ask him. Would you like me to show you how?"

Ruth nodded eagerly. Miss Charlotte took her hand and knelt with her in the soft, green grass. And there, in the quiet and beauty of the garden, Ruth gave her heart to Jesus. And just as He said He would, He turned her sorrow into joy and crying into laughter.

When they were finished, Ruth, now smiling with joy, said, "I feel so happy! I have never felt this way before! What do I do now?"

Miss Charlotte answered simply, "Share it with everyone you meet."

"Thank you, Miss Charlotte!" Ruth said as she threw her arms around her. "Thank you so much!"

As she started to rise, Miss Charlotte pressed a wrapped box into her hand.

"A birthday present," she said.

Ruth opened it eagerly.

"A Bible," she exclaimed. "Out of all the things my parents have given me, this is the best gift I have received. Thank you!"

Miss Charlotte added, "May it help you grow strong in the Lord and to keep his commandments faithfully."

A smile of gratefulness lit Ruth's pretty face as she hurried off. I can't wait to tell all the other children about my new father, Ruth thought as she hurried inside, her blue eyes shining.

Watching the new child of God run off, Miss Charlotte sighed. If only all the young orphans in the world could know of the Heavenly Father and His love for them, she thought. And with this burden in her heart, Miss Charlotte rose to finish her duties.

Entering the dormitory, Ruth was met by a group of girls that loved to mercilessly tease her.

The leader of the group, Lucy, sneered, "Well, look who's here. Little Miss Orphan. Have you been crying for your lost parents again?"

And Ruth, instead of feeling angry as before, instead felt sorry for the girls.

Going up to Lucy, Ruth put her hand on her shoulder and quietly said, "Lucy, I am sorry that you don't have any parents but can I introduce you to a father that will always be there when you need Him?"

Taken aback, Lucy stammered, "Sure, I suppose you can."

So Ruth sat down and started to tell them all about Jesus. From that time forward, the children's home was changed. There was no more teasing or ridiculing. There was only happiness and laughter, proof of what the love of God can do.

Abigail Wolking
10th Grade

Community Voice Media, LLC, is a Small Print Publishing Company Specializing in Local Anthologies

The mission of Community Voice Media is to make a positive difference in the community by providing a program of support for young writers, encouraging them to let their voices be heard.

www.communityvoicemedia.com

Community Voice Media, LLC acknowledges and appreciates the inspiration and assistance of two very special local foundations. We encourage you to learn more about their individual missions and to support them according to your personal ability.

Just For Mom Foundation

www.justformom.com
Tara Paterson, Founder

It is our goal to be a support system for the woman who needs it most-*mom*; and together with many amazing women we are going to make it possible for women to find refuge for themselves and build a business from home with helpful tools to guide them. We welcome any woman who wants to share in the growth of this exciting adventure. Our goal is to *"Touch Each Mom's Life, One Mom at a Time."*

pawsforpeoplefoundationsm

www.paws4people.com
Terry Henry, Director

The mission of the ***paws4peoplefoundation***SM is to enhance the lives of special and regular education children, seniors, and the seriously ill, by utilizing the "special powers" of canine companionship displayed by highly trained therapy dogs in specialized educational programs, therapy visitations, and private placements.

www.communityvoicemedia.com

www.bobbicarducci.com